TREASURES of TRUTH

♡

FOR A LIFE OF VICTORY

Treasures of Truth

FOR A LIFE OF VICTORY

LISA STATON

ISBN: 979-8-9926703-0-1

Scripture taken from the New King James Version®. Copyright © 1982 by Thomas Nelson. Used by permission. All rights reserved.

Scripture quotations taken from the Amplified® Bible (AMPC), Copyright © 1954, 1958, 1962, 1964, 1965, 1987 by The Lockman Foundation. Used by permission. lockman.org.

Scripture quotations marked (NLT) are taken from the Holy Bible, New Living Translation, copyright ©1996, 2004, 2015 by Tyndale House Foundation. Used by permission of Tyndale House Publishers, Carol Stream, Illinois 60188. All rights reserved.

Scriptures marked KJV are taken from the King James Version (KJV): King James Version, public domain.

Scripture taken from the Holy Bible: International Standard Version®. Copyright © 1996-forever by The ISV Foundation. All Rights Reserved Internationally. Used by permission.

Scripture quotations marked MSG are taken from The Message, copyright © 1993, 2002, 2018 by Eugene H. Peterson. Used by permission of NavPress. All rights reserved. Represented by Tyndale House Publishers.

Interior Design by Gloria Erickson, London Lane Designs, Cover Design by Julia Arambam

Published in the United States of America.

CONTENTS

INTRODUCTION

———————— ♡ ————————

Do you have questions and need answers to problems in your life? God's Word has the answers. If this sounds too good to be true, I encourage you to keep reading.

As you apply these simple messages in *Treasures of Truth*, you will see results. I have seen these truths work in my life for over 40 years, as I have received and believed them in my heart! God's Word is true, and it will not return void.

In the mid-late 80's, God opened my heart as He did with Lydia in Acts 16:14. I *heard* the message of the *simplicity* of the gospel of Jesus Christ being preached. Through the hearing of the gospel, the Lord *started* giving me a revelation of everything Jesus provided for *me* on the Cross.

Jesus says in Mark 1:15, "The time is fulfilled, and the kingdom of God is at hand. *Repent*, and *believe* the gospel." Repentance is a change of heart. I *turned from* what I was believing and thought to be true and started believing the gospel. Changes started taking place in my heart, which is where change always begins.

The gospel is defined in Romans 1:16-17 as the

power of God unto salvation to those who believe. Salvation is anything you need from the time you are born again until you go to be with the Lord. It is a word that means set at safety, delivered, healed, nothing lacking, nothing missing in your life. Verse 17 continues saying that it is in the gospel that the righteousness of God is revealed from faith to faith. The just shall *live* by faith.

Paul declared to the Corinthians in 1 Corinthians 15:1-4 the gospel; how Jesus died for our sins according to scripture, that He was buried, and that He rose again on the third day according to scripture. That is the power of God for our salvation.

With an unshakeable determination to see God's Word manifest in my life, I set my heart to believe the gospel. If God said it, I wanted to see it work in my life. The power of God started setting me free from bondages and wrong thinking as I read and renewed my mind daily.

Planting the seed of the Word into my heart was an anchor for my soul (Hebrews 6:19). Nothing could take it away; it became a *stronghold* of truth and victory. That power is still working in my life today!

The gospel is for _whosoever_ will believe – trust in, rely on, and adhere to it like super glue! God is no respecter of persons, and He has no favorites. He responds to faith – for without faith, you cannot please Him. *Whosoever* chooses to *receive and believe* this gospel will see the impossible become possible. They will see God's power work in miraculous ways.

Continual transformation has taken place in my

heart – changing me from the inside out. I have experiencec healing in my body, as well as many others I have prayed for. I have seen the dead raised, as I prayed in faith and took God at His Word (Matthew 10:8) - not what I saw with my natural eyes.

Treasures of Truth is filled with scripture and words of encouragement to ignite your faith into believing all that Jesus has provided for you. You can use this book as a devotional or as a study guide if you want to go deeper into the different topics.

As you apply the Word of God in your life, you will:

- Experience the freedom Jesus came to give you
- Become all that God created you to be
- Do all He has ordained you to do in His Kingdom

May these truths of God's love for you penetrate deep into your heart. May they become the foundation on which you stand to see the salvation of God manifest in your life daily!

A GODLY LIFE THROUGH THE KNOWLEDGE OF HIM

———————— ♡ ————————

Grace and peace be multiplied to you in the knowledge of God and of Jesus our Lord, as His divine power has given to us all things that pertain to life and godliness, through the knowledge of Him who called us by glory and virtue, by which have been given to us exceedingly great and precious promises, that through these you may be partakers of the divine nature, having escaped the corruption that is in the world through lust.

2 Peter 1:2-4 NKJV

As we learn and understand more of God and His ways, the more we can walk in the truth of His divine power and what His power provided for us through the death, burial, and resurrection of Jesus. Getting to know Him by having a personal, intimate relationship with Him is what the Christian walk is about. It allows us to partake of His exceedingly great and precious promises, which are *always* yes and amen (2 Corinthians 1:20).

As the world grows darker, the light in us will shine brighter because of the excellency of His power in these earthen vessels (2 Corinthians 4:6-7). We have on the inside of us what the world is looking for: hope, love, peace, forgiveness, healing, joy, wisdom, mercy, grace, truth, and the list goes on. We have everything we need in this life to live victoriously. We can then minister these truths to others.

What people have been taught that does not line up with God's Word is called tradition of man, which makes the Word of God of none effect (Mark 7:7-13). Only by getting to know Jesus, through His Word, can we truly be partakers of His divine nature. The more we get to know Him in a personal intimate way, the more we will escape from being conformed to the corruption and evil in this world.

If there is something in the Bible that is new to you that does not agree with how you have been taught or what you learned growing up, it will take humility to admit it. God grants grace to the humble but resists the proud (James 4:6). Pride always argues with the truth of God's Word. However, truth always prevails over lies.

Be encouraged today, and desire to walk in all the provisions that God's divine power has made available for you. May His grace and peace be multiplied to you this day!

ADJUST YOUR FOCUS

───────── ♡ ─────────

*Set your mind and keep focused habitually
on the things above (the heavenly things), not
on things that are on the earth (which have only
temporal value).*

Colossians 3:2 AMP

If we are honest, we can say at one time or another we have taken our focus off the Lord and put it on the cares and distractions of life. This is when things can turn blurry in no time. Everything starts looking bleak. Before you know it, negativity has taken over to where nothing looks good. You end up in a total state of fear, unbelief, and anxiety wondering what if this or what if that. What if, what if, what if...!

In these last days, it is imperative to keep your focus on the Word of God and His truths. You have a choice as to whether you keep it on the Lord or put your focus on what you see and hear going on around you. We are not to be like an ostrich putting our heads in the sand, neither are we to let the cares and distractions of things we hear and see take root in our hearts. That is why it says to guard our hearts with all diligence for

7

out of it (our hearts) are the issues, or wellsprings, of life (Proverbs 4:23).

When you start to see yourself getting negative and feeling hopeless, ask yourself, "Where is my focus? What am I giving my time and attention to? What lies am I believing that are against the truth of God's Word?" When you realize your focus is not on the Lord, repent and get back on track. Remember, whatever you focus on will be magnified, whether good or bad.

So, if your focus is blurry, adjust it back to the truth of God's Word and His promises!

AGAINST HOPE

―――――― ♡ ――――――

Who against hope believed in hope...

Romans 4:18 KJV

I love Romans 4 about Abraham because this is an example that can apply to any situation in our lives that looks impossible. Abraham against (contrary to) hope, believed in hope concerning the child God promised him when his body and Sarah's womb were both dead - past the age of childbearing. This was an impossible situation, BUT GOD. The promise of God came forth with Isaac being born when Abraham was 100 years old, and Sarah was 90 years old (Genesis 17:17).

The word 'hope' here means favorable and confident expectation, to anticipate or expect good. It has to do with the unseen and the future. We can read in Romans 8:24-25 NKJV, "For we were saved in this hope, but hope that is seen is not hope; for why does one still hope for what he sees? But if we hope for what we do not see, we eagerly wait for it with perseverance." We are to be joyful (rejoice and be glad) in hope.

How did this impossible, hopeless situation with Abraham come forth? In Romans 4, as you read this chapter, it says he was not weak in faith. He did not stagger (waver) at the promise of God through unbelief, even though in the natural realm there was no way possible for this to take place. He was strong in faith, knowing what God had promised, God was able to perform, and he gave glory to God. Strong faith will always glorify God in any given situation. Do you have a situation in your life right now where it is impossible in the natural realm? This should be an encouragement to all of us.

You may not see right now in the physical realm how you want your checkbook to look, how you want your body to feel, how you want your relationships to be, or even a promise God has spoken to you. But if you are in Christ, you can hope (be in confident expectation) for those things to change, and they will. This is not saying, "Well, I hope so" like many people say, when in fact, it is nothing more than doubt and unbelief. The hope it is talking about here is being confident and assured that what we do not see yet, if we persevere in faith, we will see the changes we are looking for. This was how Abraham obtained the promise of God – against hope, he believed in hope. And it came to pass.

Remember, all things are possible for those who believe!

ALL AUTHORITY HAS BEEN GIVEN TO US

———————— ♡ ————————

Behold, I give you the authority to trample on serpents and scorpions, and over all the power of the enemy, and nothing shall by any means hurt you. Nevertheless do not rejoice in this, that the spirits are subject to you, but rather rejoice because your names are written in heaven.

Luke 10:19-20 NKJV

Do we really believe we have been given *ALL* power and authority over the enemy in the name of Jesus? Do we really believe we can live a life of victory and overcome *any* attack of the enemy by trusting in and having faith in the blood of Jesus?

We, as born again believers, don't have to live a defeated, discouraged, disappointed life full of hinderances that weigh us down. We can have victory in every situation over every attack of the enemy. We have been given the name of Jesus, which is above every name that is named. It tells us in Philippians 2:10-11 that at His name every knee should bow in heaven and earth and every tongue confess that Jesus is Lord to the glory of the Father. His name is powerful!

Jesus said He has given *US* authority over serpents and scorpions and over all the power of the enemy that nothing shall by any means harm us. That means we have authority over fear, hopelessness, sin, sickness, anger, disease, addictions, or anything else that hinders us from walking in total victory. When we use our God given authority, that is the love of God in action. It is not saying the enemy won't throw things at us, but we don't have to catch anything he throws our way - not one thing.

God does give us a warning, though, not to rejoice that spirits are subject to us, but to rejoice that our names are written in the book of life. What a blessing that is!

As our key verse says, God has given US authority over all the power of the enemy. I would encourage you to use your authority. If we submit to God and resist the devil, he will flee from us (James 4:7)!

ALL OF GOD'S WAYS ARE PERFECT

───────────── ♡ ─────────────

As for God, His way is perfect; The word of the Lord is proven; He is a shield to all who trust in Him.

Psalm 18:30 NKJV

What a blessing to be able to trust God for His perfect way for our life instead of trusting our own way. The word 'perfect' means entire, integrity, truth, without blemish, complete, full, sound, without spot, undefiled, upright, whole.

When we do things God's way instead of our own, we will not make mistakes or have heartaches, disappointments, or frustrations. This is called 'being led by His Spirit'. He will lead us according to His will for our life and will be a protector over us because we are putting our trust in Him. Deuteronomy 32:4 says, "He is the Rock, His work is perfect; For all His ways are justice, a God of truth and without injustice; righteous and upright is He." (NKJV)

There may be times in your life when you think your way is the best and that God will put His stamp of approval on it. That is when you get off into deception and end up on a path of destruction. Proverbs 21:2 tells us that a man's ways seem right to him, but the Lord weighs or examines the heart. Another scripture in Proverbs 14:12 tells us that there is a way that seems right to a man, but its end is the way of death. You may think things are taking too long and you get ahead of God and get in the flesh (Genesis 16). But as it says in John 6:63, the flesh profits nothing. The bottom line is God's ways never fail - they are proven and will bring forth the best results for your life.

God's timing is always perfect as well. He is never late and rarely early! While trusting Him to lead and guide you down the path He has for your life, you will develop patience (continuance, endurance). If you will let patience have its perfect work in you, you will be perfect (complete) and entire (whole, perfectly sound), wanting (lacking) nothing (James 1:4). Wow - what a great promise that is!

When the Lord moved me and my husband to Colorado in 2015 to go to Charis Bible College, we could have said, "No that won't work - we have kids and grandkids, and we can't leave them." However, when you obey God and do things His way, He will take care of everything. Deuteronomy says you will be blessed coming in and blessed going out, you will be blessed in the city and blessed in the field. Wherever He leads you, you will be blessed and favored by Him. You will be in your place called 'there'. And you stay 'there' until He speaks or leads you elsewhere.

There is no greater or safer place to be than in God's perfect will doing life His way. Every provision you need will be provided in your place called 'there'!

ARE YOU AFRAID?

———————— ♡ ————————

What time I am afraid, I will trust in thee. In God I will praise his word, in God I have put my trust: I will not fear what flesh can do unto me.

Psalm 56:3-4 KJV

There are opportunities in life to be afraid. There may be fear of the future and what it holds for you. There may be fear of losing your job or of lack in your finances. There may be fear for your children with all the evil going on in today's world. There could be a fear of heights, a fear of dying, or even a fear of what people can do to you. It could be any number of things. Being afraid of something or someone will hold you back and keep you from seeing victory in these areas.

In this verse, God says what time we are afraid, we will put our trust IN HIM and take refuge IN HIM. Your confidence will be IN HIM. You can be bold and secure IN HIM and put your hope IN HIM. When you sense fear gripping your heart, speak out the promises of God and declare what He says, not the thoughts and feelings you are experiencing.

We know from 2 Timothy 1:7 that fear is a spirit

and God did not give it to us. It is not that fear won't come knocking at our door or that we won't have opportunities to be afraid, because we will. But we can say when it comes, "My trust is IN God; my confidence is IN HIM. HE is my shield and my buckler; HE is my refuge and strength in time of trouble; HE is my provider and healer."

Just as fear paralyzes faith, know that faith paralyzes fear. As born again believers, God has given us *the measure of faith* (Romans 12:3). We can overcome all fear in our lives by allowing the love of God to be perfected in us because the perfect love of God casts out all fear (1 John 4:18).

Decide today that what time you are afraid, *you will* put your confidence and trust in the Lord. Decide that *you will* put your trust in what His Word says over whatever fear is knocking at your door. Another powerful weapon against the enemy is to praise God. It tells us in the Word that perfect praise stills the enemy and avenger. Learn to praise God when these tactics of the enemy come knocking at your door and watch him flee.

God's Word always works when WE put it to work!

ARISE AND SHINE

———— ♡ ————

Arise, shine; For your light has come! And the glory of the Lord is risen upon you. For behold, the darkness shall cover the earth, and deep darkness the people; But the Lord will arise over you, And His glory will be seen upon you.

Isaiah 60:1-2 NKJV

In the above verses, Isaiah prophesied exactly what we are seeing today in this dark and evil world. It is getting darker for people that walk in darkness. But the Lord will shine upon those of us who are believers in Christ; those who know their God and trust Him.

People have choices to make every day that will affect whether they go God's way or the world's way. The world's path is full of darkness and evil, which will end in destruction. People that choose that destructive path call evil good and good evil. They are blinded by the god of this world, the devil.

It says in Acts 26:18 that people are either in darkness or light, either following Satan's power or the power of God. However, God has *given us the choice* of who we will follow and serve. He is a gentleman, and He will not force us to obey Him. We can choose to have blessings or curses; we can choose good or evil; we can choose life or death. In Deuteronomy 30:15-20, God gives us the answer and wants us to choose life. He wants us to walk in His blessings and His goodness, but the choice is still ours to make. It comes down to obedience or disobedience. Which one will you choose?

If you will let God's light shine in and through you, there will be people in darkness who will see there is something different about you and want it. Of course, not everyone wants the light. Many people who practice evil hate the light and don't want their evil deeds exposed, as it tells us in John 3:20. However, there will be people who come to the truth because of the light that is shining in and through you and me.

As believers, God has chosen us for such a time as this. So let your light shine and know that the glory of the Lord is risen upon you to have an impact on people that are in darkness!

BE AN OVERCOMER

———————— ♡ ————————

*For whatever is born of God overcomes the
world. And this is the victory that has overcome
the world – our faith.*

1 John 5:4 NKJV

To overcome means to conquer, prevail, or get
victory. Do you have anything in your life right now
that you need to get victory over? We all do! There is
hope because God says we are overcomers in this life
because greater is He in us, than he (the enemy) who
is in the world (1 John 4:4).

Anything in our life that does not align with the
truth of God's Word, we can overcome. For example,
if you have sickness in your body, you can choose to
believe God to receive the healing that Jesus provided
for you. If there is unforgiveness in your heart towards
someone, you can overcome it by choosing to forgive
that person because Jesus has forgiven you. It is a
choice whether we will be overcomers or *be overcome.*

In the book of Revelation, it says things about overcomers – such as how to overcome and what the
overcomers will receive. Revelation 12:10-11 states,

"Then I heard a loud voice saying in heaven, "Now salvation, and strength, and the kingdom of our God, and the power of His Christ have come, for the accuser of our brethren, who accused them before our God day and night, has been cast down. And they overcame him by the blood of the Lamb and by the word of their testimony, and they did not love their lives to the death." (NKJV)

What a blessing that we can overcome when we speak our testimony with courage and boldness because of the blood of the Lamb and not love our lives unto death. Praise God, He has given us a way to gain the victory over whatever hinderances or obstacles are in our way.

Everything that the enemy wants to do in our lives, (which is steal, kill, and destroy - John 10:10), we can overcome because Jesus *has already* overcome; and the victory for us to overcome is *our* faith.

It also tells us in Revelation 21:7 that he who overcomes shall inherit all things, and God will be our God, and we shall be His sons. There are other things in the book of Revelation that talk about the overcomers, which I will briefly list below. It begins by saying, "To those who have ears to hear, let them hear what the Spirit is saying."

Those who overcome:

- He will grant us to eat of the tree of life, which is in the midst of the paradise of God – Revelation 2:7
- We will not be hurt by the second death

– Revelation 2:11

- He will give us to eat of the hidden manna, and a white stone, and a new name written on the stone which no man knows but the one who receives it – Revelation 2:17
- He will give us power over the nations – Revelation 2:26
- He will clothe us in white garments, and will not erase our name from the book of life, but will confess our name before the Father and His angels – Revelation 3:5
- He will make us a pillar in the temple of our God, and we will not go out from it anymore; and He will write on us the name of our God, and the name of the city of our God, the new Jerusalem, which comes down out of heaven from our God, and His new name – Revelation 3:12
- He will grant us to sit down with Him on His throne, just as He sat down with the Father on His throne – Revelation 3:21
- We shall inherit all things – Revelation 21:7

Romans 12:21 in the Amplified version tells us, "Do not be overcome and conquered by evil, but overcome evil with good." Romans 8:31, 37 says if God is for us, who can be against us because we are more than conquerors through Him who loved us.

There are biblical examples of overcoming evil with good, such as, instead of cursing those who persecute you, bless them. Pray for those who despitefully use you. If your enemy is hungry, give him food to eat, if he is thirsty, give him water to drink. If you are in fear (which is evil, it is not of God), God says perfect love will cast out all fear. Ask God to give you a revelation of His love for you, and you will overcome fear.

Remember, whatever evil is present in your life or coming against you, you can overcome it because Jesus has already overcome!

BE STILL AND KNOW
THAT I AM GOD

———————— ♡ ————————

*Be still, and know that I am God: I will be
exalted among the heathen, I will be exalted in
the earth.*

Psalm 46:10 (KJV)

It is so important that we learn to quieten ourselves (be still) before the Lord and know (get acquainted with, acknowledge, be aware) that God is God, and we are not. When we come to that place in our hearts, which is a place of rest, there will be no pressure or turmoil over anything going on in our lives, or in the world, that would otherwise make us fretful and anxious.

It goes on in the rest of this verse saying that He will be exalted among the heathen, He will be exalted in the earth. No flesh is going to glory in His presence (1 Corinthians 1:29).

We serve an awesome God who *only* has good for His people. He cares so much about us and wants us to surrender our lives totally to Him and let Him be the ruler of our hearts in every situation. He wants us

25

to let Him be God in our lives, not us be our own god.

Anxiety, fear, unbelief, unsettledness, unquietness - they should have no access or place in our hearts and lives as believers. Why? Because we are more than conquerors. We will always triumph and get victory over every circumstance that arises against us if we stand fast and believe God.

So today, be still and quieten your heart and know (be aware) that God is God. As you trust Him in whatever it is you are going through, you will go through in victory to the other side!

BEING CONFORMED TO HIS IMAGE

———————— ♡ ————————

For whom He foreknew, He also predestined
to be conformed to the image of His Son, that
He might be the firstborn among many brethren.

Romans 8:29 NKJV

To be conformed to the image of Jesus is the will of God for our lives. We need to ask ourselves, "Is this happening in my life? Am I conforming to HIS image or am I being conformed to the image of the world?"

Let's look at what some of the words mean in Romans 8:29:

Foreknew - to know beforehand, ordain before

Predestinated - to determine before; foreordain, mark out beforehand

Conformed - fashioned like unto another; having the same form as another; similar, jointly formed

Image - representation, resemblance

Those that God knew beforehand, He foreordained to be fashioned in His resemblance. The more we walk with the Lord in our daily lives, the more we should be representing His character. We should be conforming to His ways, His truths, His love, His peace, His righteousness, His joy, among other things. This is a process, so we should not allow the enemy to condemn us. When we see that we are not exemplifying His character, we can repent and ask God to perfect our love.

It is His life that we should be imitating as Paul said in Ephesians 5:1-2, "Imitate God, therefore, in everything you do, because you are His dear children. Live a life filled with love following the example of Christ. He loved us and offered Himself as a sacrifice for us, a pleasing aroma to God." (NLT)

As Paul told the church in 1 Corinthians 11:1 (KJV), "Be ye followers of me, even as I also am of Christ." If we say we abide in Him, we ought to be walking like He walked – 1 John 2:6. How did Jesus walk? He went about doing good and showing compassion by healing the sick, raising the dead, casting out devils, teaching and preaching the gospel of the Kingdom, and setting the captives free.

In Ephesians 2:10 it tells us that we are His workmanship, created in Christ Jesus unto good works, which God has before ordained (prepared) that we should walk in them. God's plan for our lives is to be an ambassador for Christ demonstrating His power to others (2 Corinthians 5:20). There is no greater joy and honor than to be a representative for the Lord while here on this earth!

BENEFITS OF BLESSING THE LORD

──────────── ♡ ────────────

Who forgives all your iniquities, who heals all your diseases, who redeems your life from destruction, who crowns you with lovingkindness and tender mercies, who satisfies your mouth with good things, so that your youth is renewed like the eagle's.

Psalm 103:3-5 NKJV

I would encourage you to read this whole chapter as it has so many good things in it.

In the first couple of verses, it tells us twice to "bless the Lord, oh my soul." As it goes on in the rest of verse 2, it says we are *not* to forget any of the Lord's benefits. Yes, the Lord has benefits for us, and we need to constantly remember what they are.

The benefits that God has for us far outweigh anything the world has to offer, and His benefits are free! Jesus paid for every one of these benefits. He did it for you and me because of His unconditional love for us. Nothing can compare to them.

These benefits allow us to walk in *FREEDOM FROM*

sin, sickness, disease, and destruction. His loving-kindness and tender mercies encircle us. That is a blessing for sure!

We can have our youth renewed as the eagles, as it says in verse 5. Eagles fly above the storms, not under them. That is where the Lord wants us to be – above and not beneath the storms of life. Then we will be in a place of rest instead of turmoil. The eagles have strong vision and focus. They can see an object or prey up to 3 miles away, and they will not take their focus from it until they have succeeded in capturing it. We should have an unobstructed vision of what the Lord has for us and stay focused on it until His will is accomplished in our life.

The eagles also only eat fresh prey - nothing dead. Are we feasting on fresh manna of the Word of God daily and getting fresh revelation from it? Or are we feeding on the cares of this world, which produce death, not life? It tells us in Isaiah 40:31 that if we wait (expect) upon the Lord, our strength will be renewed. We will mount up with wings like eagles; we will run and not be weary, we will walk and not faint. That is renewed youth!

What amazing promises God has provided for His people. I would encourage you to taste and see that the Lord is good. Trust in His benefits for your life, as you bless Him with all your soul!

BLESSED IS SHE THAT BELIEVED

———————— ♡ ————————

Blessed is she who believed, for there will be a fulfillment of those things which were told her from the Lord.

Luke 1:45 NKJV

How many of you have a promise, or promises, that God has spoken to you that have not yet been fulfilled? I know I do.

As I was praying one day about one specific promise and was putting God in remembrance of what He had said to me (Isaiah 43:26), I also thanked *Him for bringing it to pass*. I then heard Him speak the above scripture to me.

God gave me a dream about this promise in early 2020. As soon as I woke up, I heard Him *say* the exact same thing I heard Him tell me in the dream. This promise is far bigger than anything I can do to bring it to pass. That is good because only God will get the glory for performing it. When we can do things in and of our own strength or power, then there is no place for God to get the glory. Only when it is bigger than what *we're* capable of can we be assured it is God.

1 Corinthians 1:29 says that NO FLESH will glory in His presence. If we can perform the promise, it is flesh and not God. Philippians 3:3 says we are to have *no* confidence in the flesh. If flesh gets in the way, it will have a totally different outcome, as we know with Abraham.

When Abraham tried to speed up the process concerning the child God had promised him and Sarah, he ended up having a child that was not with Sarah and not the will of God. In Romans 4, we can see that God brought Abraham's heart to a place of repentance where he was fully persuaded that what *God* had promised, *God* would perform. Abraham got unbelief (self/flesh) out of the way.

Faith always has corresponding actions associated with it (James 2). However, God will lead you and show you what those steps are. God is always willing and ready to perform His Word in our lives. But there is also 'His timing' where everything must be aligned for it to work. There may be a divine appointment or divine connection that God has for you that is crucial in bringing the promise to pass.

It reminds me of a puzzle. It is placing one piece at a time in the puzzle. Every piece must be in its proper place for the puzzle to be completed. As we take each step He directs, it will bring us closer and closer to obtaining what He has promised and spoken to us – which is a completed or manifested promise!

BY HIS STRIPES YOU WERE AND ARE HEALED

———— ♡ ————

Isaiah 53:5 and 1 Peter 2:24

Did you know that Jesus paid for YOUR healing on the cross so that you do not have to be sick or if you get sick you can be healed?

Isaiah 53:5 tells us that with the stripes that Jesus bore on His body on the cross, we ARE healed (this was a prophecy looking to the cross). And 1 Peter 2:24 (looking back to the cross) says we WERE healed (2000 years ago).

When Jesus took those stripes on His back on the cross, He said, "It is finished." Every sin, sickness, and disease was placed upon His body. An exchange was made so we could have His righteousness for our sin, divine health or healing if we get sick. He paid the price for this exchange with His own blood that He shed on the cross. That is how much He loves us. (Read all His benefits in Psalm 103:1-5).

You may be thinking, "Well, if He healed everyone, why isn't everyone healed and walking in it?" The answer is simple - you must believe and receive it by faith for the manifestation to come forth. Grace (Jesus) provided it, but Faith (our part) must receive it.

Just as God sent His One and Only Son to die, be buried, and be raised again the third day so that people could be born again and have everlasting life, not everyone is born again. You must do what it says in Romans 10:9-10 (NKJV), "...that if you confess with your mouth the Lord Jesus and believe in your heart that God has raised Him from the dead, you will be saved. For with the heart, one believes unto righteousness, and with the mouth confession is made unto salvation." We have a part to play and that is *believing* what Jesus (Grace) did for us and *receiving* it by faith.

The question is, where is your trust when things start happening that are not good in your life, such as sickness and disease? Do you turn to the ways of the world, or do you turn to the One who has the answer and paid for your healing with His life? There is absolutely no condemnation to going to a doctor, but there is a better way. That way is believing God for your healing which was provided on the Cross.

Any problem we encounter in this life, the answer is found in the Word of God. The Word of God is a blueprint for our life. It must be accessed by faith. The answer is *always* victory through faith in the blood of Jesus. He always causes us to triumph in Christ Jesus (2 Corinthians 2:14).

I would encourage you to trust in the Lord with all your heart and not lean to your own understanding. If you acknowledge Him in all your ways, He will direct your path (Proverbs 3:5-6). Start today believing Him in small things that are going on in your life so when the storms of life come (and they will), your anchor and trust will be in God alone!

CASTING YOUR CARES

———————— ♡ ————————

Therefore humble yourselves under the mighty hand of God, that He may exalt you in due time, casting all your care upon Him, for He cares for you.

1 Peter 5:6-7 NKJV

What cares are you carrying today?

In these verses, God is wanting us to 'throw' our cares on Him because He cares for us. Cares can be worries, fears or anxiety, or any type of distraction that gets our focus off the Lord and onto our problems.

In Matthew 13:22, where Jesus is talking about the parable of the Sower, He says that the cares of the world, along with the deceitfulness of riches, choke the Word and it becomes unfruitful. Cares will cause God's Word to be drowned, or choked, out of your heart to keep you from bearing fruit or seeing results in your life.

These distractions can never change the situation. That is why God gives us instructions on what to do with them. They do not belong to us. He does not want us carrying them because they will shut up our faith and hinder the power of God from producing victory in our life. The very things you are anxious or worried about will not be resolved by hanging onto them. However, when you give them to God, it is an act of humility, and it is obedience to His Word.

Psalm 55:22 tells us to cast our burden upon the Lord because He will sustain us. It tells us that He will never allow the righteous to be moved. So let go of these distractions and do some 'casting' today, and watch God move on your behalf!

CLAY IN THE POTTER'S HAND

———————— ♡ ————————

*And yet, O Lord, you are our Father. We are the
clay, and you are the potter. We all are formed
by your hand.*

Isaiah 64:8 NLT

We are like clay in our Master's hand, being formed
into His masterpiece to do what He has called us to do.

In Romans 8:29, "For whom He did foreknow, He
also did predestinate to be conformed to the image
of His Son..." (KJV)

It says in 2 Timothy 2:20-21, "But in a great house
there are not only vessels of gold and silver, but also
of wood and of earth: and some to honour, and some
to dishonour. If a man therefore purge himself from
these, he shall be a vessel unto honour, sanctified, and
meet for the master's use, and prepared unto every
good work." (KJV)

That word prepared (to be made ready) is one that
most people do not like, especially when you are the
one going through it. However, when you understand
it is a process that is for your good, it does make it

somewhat easier! As we have all heard, preparation time is *never* wasted time.

As believers, we will go through times of preparation being put on the wheel, so to speak, to be shaped and molded. This will be according to His purpose and grace that was ordained before the world began.

Just as clay has water added to it to make it pliable and soft so that it can be put on the wheel and formed to be useful (Jeremiah 18), so it is with us when we allow the water of the Word to wash us (Ephesians 5:26). It allows our hearts to be made pliable for what God wants to do with us.

It also tells us in Jeremiah 23:29 that His Word is as a fire and as a hammer that breaks the rocks into pieces. When our hearts are hardened by the deceitfulness of sin, the Word of God will be as a hammer and as a fire. It will break out that hardness to where it will be softened, so we will be willing to obey God's calling and purpose for our lives. He will take out our stony heart and give us a heart of flesh, as it says in Ezekiel 36:26.

There are times when we will go through the fire to have our faith tested and tried (1 Peter 1:7), just as the clay pot is put in a kiln to make it strong and firm. Our faith, which is more precious than gold, will come out on the other side, resulting in praise, honor, and glory at the revelation of Jesus Christ. Remember, we are clay in the Potter's hand – we are the work of His hand!

DECLARING THE END FROM THE BEGINNING

———— ♡ ————

Declaring the end from the beginning, and
from ancient times things that are not yet done,
saying, "My counsel shall stand, and I will do all
My pleasure."

Isaiah 46:10 NKJV

Whatever is happening in your life today, God knows the end of your situation from the beginning. He knows that the truth will prevail, and victory will come forth, if you believe Him.

The sooner we align ourselves with His truth about the situation (what the Word says), the sooner we will see it come forth. Too many times, we believe what we see, think, or feel in the natural realm over what the Word of God says about our situation in the spiritual realm. We end up staying stuck there longer than necessary.

Isaiah 55:11 tells us that God's Word will never return void. When we begin to declare what God is declaring over the situation we are walking through, our soul will begin to line up with what is true in the Spirit. Then these things will manifest in the natural realm. God's timing does have something to do with it in certain incidences. When we get our focus off 'how long' something is going to take and instead give Him thanks that He is working, we will see results we are believing for come forth sooner. Keep speaking and declaring, knowing God is at work.

As a reminder, the children of Israel wandered in the wilderness for 40 years, and it was only an 11-day journey to the promised land. That would be disheartening. They murmured and complained even though they saw God do one miracle after another for them, which is a hard heart. They died in the wilderness and never entered the promised land. Having a thankful heart will always produce God's results in your life over complaining and murmuring.

God is merciful, gracious, and longsuffering. He knows how long it will take to get our hearts to a place of change, or repentance; and He will never give up on us. That is the unconditional love of God. It does not do any good to look back and regret because things took so long. Just be thankful when your heart comes to the light and correction takes place.

Declare God's truth over your situation and watch and see His salvation manifest in your life!

DON'T QUIT – DON'T GIVE UP

———— ♡ ————

*And let us not grow weary while doing good,
for in due season we shall reap if we do not
lose heart.*

Galatians 6:9 NKJV

Many times, when we almost have the victory, we quit and throw in the towel. We become weary in our souls (mind, will, and emotions). The enemy tries to put more pressure on us to bring us to the point of giving up and giving in to what he wants instead of what God has for us.

Jesus told us not to be weary (to be utterly spiritless, to be exhausted, faint in your heart, lose or lack courage, be weak) in well doing, for He said we would reap in due season (right or opportune time), if we don't faint.

If you need a breakthrough, DON'T QUIT NOW. Usually right before the breakthrough is when it seems darkest. But there is light at the end of the tunnel. God is faithful to get you to the other side in victory. He has already paid the price for whatever it is you need to see come forth. Set your heart and mind on Him and give Him thanks for what you believe to see take place. Whether it is a situation on your job, in your finances, a new opportunity, your next step, healing for your body, or whatever else it might be, set your heart on the things above and not on your circumstances.

An encouraging scripture is Isaiah 41:10 where it tells us, "Fear thou not; for I am with thee: be not dismayed; for I am thy God: I will strengthen thee; yea, I will help thee; yea, I will uphold thee with the right hand of my righteousness." (KJV)

When you have God on your side working on your behalf, there is nothing you can come up against that can defeat you – unless you stop believing Him. Unbelief is evil and it will harden your heart faster than anything. But praise God, we can repent (make a complete turnaround) and start believing again and see the salvation of God come forth.

Know that God wants to bring you to the other side of whatever it is you are needing or wanting in your life. He is faithful to get you there. Start worshipping and praising Him for His mercy, grace, and goodness.

Know this, whatever He has started in your life, He will finish it if you stay the course!

FAITH AS A MUSTARD SEED

───────────── ♡ ─────────────

Then the disciples came to Jesus privately and said, "Why could we not cast it out?" So Jesus said to them, "Because of your unbelief; for assuredly, I say to you, if you have faith as a mustard seed, you will say to this mountain, 'Move from here to there,' and it will move; and nothing will be impossible for you."

Matthew 17:19-20 NKJV

A mustard seed is the smallest of all seeds and when it is grown it is larger than all garden plants and becomes a tree (Matthew 13). Jesus tells us that if we have faith as a grain of a mustard seed, we can speak to the mountain (our problem), and it will move; and nothing shall be impossible to us.

Any mountain in our life that is hindering us from walking in the fullness of the gospel is rooted in a lack of the revelation of God's love for us and unbelief – not a lack of faith. Romans 12:3 tells us that God has given us *the measure of faith* (to born again believers). And it is faith *which works* through love.

What mountain do you need to speak to today? Is it sickness in your body? Is it bitterness or resentment towards someone? Is it fear that has you paralyzed? Is it money you need to pay bills? You do not have to put up with it for another minute. God has given _you_ the authority to speak to your mountain (your problem), and command it to bow.

There may be mountains that have weighed you down for years. If you will believe and receive what God's Word says over your situation and start speaking to your mountain instead of speaking to God about your mountain, you will see results. Use the faith God has given you. It is like a muscle – it needs to be exercised. Faith always is voice activated (it speaks), faith always has corresponding actions, and faith always works through love.

Remember, the victory that overcomes the world (any problem in your life) is YOUR faith!

FIND REST FOR YOUR SOUL

———— ♡ ————

Come to Me, all you who labor and are heavy laden, and I will give you rest. Take My yoke upon you and learn from Me, for I am gentle and lowly in heart, and you will find rest for your souls. For My yoke is easy and My burden is light.

Matthew 11:28-30 NKJV

Do you need to find rest for your soul (your mind, will, and emotions)?

Jesus is saying to you today, "Come unto Me, all you that labor (to feel fatigue, toil, be wearied), and are heavy laden (overburdened, loaded up, having spiritual anxiety), and I will give you rest (to refresh, take ease)."

Does this sound too good to be true? Whatever Jesus says is not only true, but it is also possible and available for you to obtain and walk in, *if* you will believe Him.

God knew from the beginning the struggles we would have in this life. He made a way to bring us through those struggles in victory. For many people, life can be a constant struggle. It can be a daily grind.

People learn to cope with these things. The thing is, we do not have to *cope* with anything - we can overcome (gain the victory over) everything. We are overcomers!

1 John 5:4 tells us that the victory that overcomes the world is *your* faith. *Your* faith mixed with the gospel, which is His power, (Hebrews 4:2) will overcome anything you are facing. How do I know? Because I've been there and seen it work every time by doing what these verses say. There was a time in my life that looked so dark in the natural realm that it seemed there was no way out - BUT GOD! Thank God for His Word and that if we apply it in faith, it will work. Jesus is saying to you today to come to Him to find rest for your souls. The word 'come' means to follow Him. He goes on in this verse and tells us to take His yoke (joining two things together) and learn (get to know, to observe, understand) from Him. It continues, "for I am meek (gentle and humble) and lowly (lowliness of mind, humble, cast down, of low degree) in heart."

Jesus knows where you are, and He knows what you're going through. Hebrews 4:15-16 tells us that we do not have a High Priest that cannot be touched with the feeling of our infirmities. He was tempted in ALL points like we are, *yet without sin*. Because of this, we can come boldly to His throne of grace to obtain mercy and find grace to help in time of need.

In Exodus 33, when Moses was leading the children of Israel out of Egypt into the wilderness, they were murmuring and complaining against Moses because it was so hard. Imagine the weight and pressure Moses was experiencing. The Lord talks to Moses and tells him he knows his name and that he has found grace in His sight. Then in Exodus 33:13-14, Moses says to the Lord, "Now, therefore, I pray, if I have found grace in your sight, show me now Your way, that I may know You and that I may find grace in Your sight. And consider that this nation is Your people. And He said, "My presence will go with you, and I will give you rest." (NKJV)

Did you know the presence of the Lord is with you, even in the hard times you are going through? He says He will never leave you nor forsake you (Hebrews 13:5). If you can believe this, you will enter His rest when you cease from your own works. This is called trust. Did you know you can have that kind of trust in the Lord where you rely on His strength, His peace, and His rest when the storms of life are going on all around you? Come to Jesus and cast (throw) all your cares and burdens upon Him (1 Peter 5:7). Know that He loves you and wants to give you the rest you need for your tired and weary soul this very day. His yoke is easy, and His burden is light!

GOD HAS NOT GIVEN
YOU A SPIRIT OF FEAR

— ♡ —

*For God has not given us a spirit of fear, but
of power and of love and of a sound mind.*

2 Timothy 1:7 NKJV

Fear is something I know much about. For years that spirit kept me in bondage, although at the time I didn't know it was a spirit. One thing I know is that it paralyzes faith and keeps you in bondage from experiencing what God has for your life. My fear was speaking in public, but your fear may be different.

Truths about fear:

- Fear is not from God (verse above)
- Fear is a spirit (verse above)
- Fear is bondage (Hebrews 2:15)
- Fear has torment (1 John 4:18)
- Fear is cast out by perfect love (1 John 4:18)

The devil is intentional. If you don't know how to be aware of his methods and schemes and overcome them by faith, they will take you captive and put you in bondage and keep you there. That is exactly what happened to me. Fear kept me paralyzed for years until one day, I finally knew it was right to face my fear of public speaking and start overcoming it. Faith always has corresponding actions. Another truth about fear is it's focused on 'self' and not on the living God.

So, when I was asked to speak in public years later, I knew the time had come to take a step of faith and overcome what had paralyzed me for years. That was the *beginning* of getting the victory over this spirit. I would encourage you to read 1 John 4:15-18 and see that God's love has no fear. Ask God to give you a revelation of His unconditional love for you. Once you start getting a revelation of His love on the inside of you, fear will start loosing its grip on your life.

Know that whatever fears might be plaguing you today, God wants you free. Just be willing to humble yourself and take that first step, whatever that step may be for you. Trust God, and watch and see what He does. He will meet you right where you are and grant you the grace you need to overcome. And He will perfect your love in the process.

We serve a faithful and mighty God!

GOD IS GREATLY TO BE PRAISED

———————— ♡ ————————

Great is the Lord, and greatly to be praised;
and his greatness is unsearchable.

Psalm 145:3 KJV

When you genuinely believe how great the Lord is, praise will come out of your heart and mouth so effortlessly. I know that His praises are continually coming up out of me because nothing compares to Him. I am so grateful to Him and the price He paid for my life. His mighty acts and greatness are without limit, and He is always wanting to show forth His power and majesty towards us so that we, in turn, can show it to others.

When we take the limits off God, we will stand in awe at His presence, glory, and splendor. We will be able to say, "Come and see what the Lord has done; it is marvelous in our eyes."

Praise does so many wonderful things when it comes from the heart:

- It stills the enemy and avenger
- God inhabits our praises
- We triumph in the praises of God

- It brings glory to God
- It puts off heaviness
- It is a weapon against the enemy
- It is a type of prayer
- It brings heaven down to earth
- It gets us in His presence when we enter His gates with thanksgiving and His courts with praise

Praise is a powerful tool in the believer's life. When our hearts are full of praise, things will happen. We will see things we've been believing for come to pass. God loves a heart that is full of thanksgiving and praise. Even though our flesh doesn't always feel like praising God, if we will do it regardless of how we feel, it is considered a sacrifice of praise. This glorifies God.

Remember, we serve a great and mighty God who is worthy of all praise, glory, and honor. Let the high praises of God be in your mouth continually!

GOD IS LOVE

———— ♡ ————

Dear friends, let us continue to love one another, for love comes from God. Anyone who loves is a child of God and knows God. But anyone who does not love does not know God, for God is love.

1 John 4:7-8 NLT

God does not *have* love - God *IS* love. That is His nature. The foundation for everything that we need in this life comes from a revelation of His love *for us*.

Here are some things (and there are many others) about God's love; what it is and what it will do in our lives as we trust Him and let Him work His love in and through us.

God's love:

- Is unconditional
- It is everlasting - it has no end
- Never fails
- It is pure
- Covers a multitude of sins

- Gives life and life more abundantly
- Guides us unto the end of our life
- Washes us white as snow
- Cleanses us from ALL unrighteousness
- Clothes us in a robe of righteousness
- Removes our sins as far as the east is from the west - never to be remembered again
- Heals us (if we get sick)
- Gives us divine health (in place of sickness and disease)
- Casts out all our fears
- Makes us bold as a lion
- Makes us courageous
- Will never be separated from us
- Corrects us for our profit and good
- Gives us peace like a river during any storm that life brings
- Promotes us
- Provides for all our needs and the desires He places in us
- Protects us from all evil
- Always causes us to triumph
- Turns what the enemy intends for evil into good
- Turns mourning into joy
- Gives hope where there seems to be no hope
- Takes the impossible and makes it possible
- Binds up the broken hearted

- Makes a way where there seems to be no way
- Rejoices over us with joy
- Causes us to soar like the eagle (above the storms of life)
- Gives us joy unspeakable and fullness of glory
- Gives us favor with God and man

Whatever you are going through, LOVE will bring you through in victory whether it be spiritually, mentally, physically, relationally, emotionally, or financially. Love never fails. When you are walking in the love of God, you will never fail – that is a promise!

GOD WANTS YOU TO THRIVE – NOT JUST SURVIVE?

———————— ♡ ————————

The Lord knows the days of the upright, and their inheritance shall be forever. They shall not be ashamed in the evil time, and in the days of famine they shall be satisfied.

Psalm 37:18-19 NKJV

If you are living in survival mode, you are living below how God intended for you to live. You are limiting God for the life He has already provided for you, which is His best. Those limits need to come off. In Isaiah, it tells us the children of Israel tempted and limited the Holy One of Israel.

We've all put limits on God by our wrong thinking. The way to know if you're limiting God is by seeing in His Word what all He has made available for you. Then ask yourself, "Am I living in all that He has provided for me, which is His best and more than enough?"

With all the economic turmoil that people face in the world, some people settle for, "That's just how it's going to be. We'll just have to make the best of it and even do without." Quite honestly, I do not know how people survive that don't know the Lord because without Him, there is no hope. It is Christ IN us, the hope of glory (Colossians 1:27).

God has made a way for us to thrive – not just survive. It is by trusting Him and looking to Him as our provider; not to our bank accounts, our jobs, our 401k's, or savings accounts, nor our stocks and bonds, which can all come to nothing in a moment of time. Then where is your trust and faith going to be? As our key verse says to the upright, even in evil times and days of famine or lack, we shall be satisfied.

2 Corinthians 8:9 in the NLT states, "You know the generous grace of our Lord Jesus Christ. Though He was rich, yet for your sakes He became poor, so that by His poverty He could make you rich." This is a promise of what Jesus did for you and me on the cross. There was an exchange made.

Being able to thrive is like healing or forgiveness or anything else you receive from Him – you believe what He says and receive it by faith. Faith is simply a response to what God has already provided. Faith is believing it before you see it manifest in the natural. You must decide that no matter what you see in your checkbook, what little you may have in your savings account, what hard times you may be experiencing, you are going to look to God and His Word and believe that rather than what you see with your eyes. That is faith; and faith calls things that are not as though they were (Romans 4:17).

Prosperity is not just about finances. It is walking in all that God has for you in EVERY area of your life.

Then you will be thriving and not just surviving. You will be prospering n your relationships, in your job, in your health, among other areas in your life. It tells us in 3 John 2 NKJV, "Beloved, I pray that you may prosper in *all* things and be in health, just as your soul prospers." Having a prosperous soul (mind, will, and emotions) is tied to financial prosperity as well as being healthy.

Isaiah 58:11 says, "The Lord will guide you continually, and satisfy your soul in drought, and strengthen your bones; You shall be like a watered garden, and like a spring of water, whose waters do not fail." (NKJV)

So, yes, even in tough times when the rest of the world is coming apart, you can thrive and not just survive. It is having that child-like faith that if God says it, you believe Him.

God is the only One who can make a way in the wilderness and provide water in the parched and dry places. Like our key verse says in the NLT, "Day by day the Lord takes care of the innocent, and they will receive an inheritance that lasts forever. They will not be disgraced in hard times; even in famine they will have *more than enough*." I love that. We serve a faithful God!

GODLINESS WITH CONTENTMENT

Now godliness with contentment is great gain. For we brought nothing into this world, and it is certain we can carry nothing out. And having food and clothing, with these we shall be content.

1 Timothy 6:6-8 NKJV

Godliness (holiness, reverence, respect towards God) with contentment (sufficiency, satisfaction with what one has) is great gain (exceeding acquisition or wealth). How many people think that the definition of true wealth is based upon one's possessions? How many people think that when one has achieved a certain level of success with all their possessions, only then can they truly be content, or satisfied? This scripture defines wealth as godliness with contentment.

A key word in these verses we need to focus on is godliness – having a respect and reverence towards God. When there is reverence towards Him, and we are truly satisfied and thankful for what we have, that is great gain. Jesus isn't opposed to us having things, but He is opposed to things having us. There is a significant difference! It tells us in 1 Timothy 6:10-11 that the *love* of money is the root of all evil and to flee from covetousness and loving money and follow righteousness, *godliness*, faith, love, patience, and meekness.

Jesus clearly gives a warning in Luke 12:15 NKJV saying, "Take heed and beware of covetousness, for one's life does *not* consist in the abundance of the things he possesses." The NLT says it like this, "Then he said, "Beware! Guard against every kind of greed. Life is not measured by how much you own."

The more things you obtain through the flesh instead of allowing the Spirit of God to bring them to you, the more your heart will be set on the things and not on the living God.

When you love, trust, and respect the One who will freely give you all things to enjoy, you won't have to go seeking the things – they will come to you because you are seeking first His Kingdom and His righteousness (Matthew 6:33)!

GOD'S WORD IN YOUR LIFE

─────────── ♡ ───────────

So shall My Word be that goes forth from My mouth; it shall not return to Me void, but it shall accomplish what I please, and it shall prosper in the thing for which I sent it.

Isaiah 55:11 NKJV

This is what the Word of God says in scripture that it will do in your life:

- It is like a hammer – it will break out the stony places in your heart
- It is like a fire – it will burn out the chaff
- It is like a sword – it will discern the thoughts and intents of the heart, dividing between the soul and spirit
- It is like a mirror – it reflects who you are in Christ
- It is like light – it will brighten your path
- It is like rain and snow – it will water your soul
- It is like silver and gold – it is precious, valuable, and pure

- It is a lamp and a guide – it will lead you in the right way
- It is like medicine – it will bring healing to your soul and body
- It is like a seed – it will produce results if planted in your heart
- It is like honey and the honeycomb – it is sweet to the taste
- It is like milk - it will nourish you and cause you to grow
- It is like food – it will strengthen you and satisfy your hunger
- It is like water – it will quench your thirst
- It is like soap – it will cleanse you (from the inside out!)

The Word of God is every one of the things listed above and so much more!

GOD'S WORD IS ALIVE AND POWERFUL

———————— ♡ ————————

For the word of God is living and powerful, and sharper than any two-edged sword, piercing even to the division of soul and spirit, and of joints and marrow, and is a discerner of the thoughts and intents of the heart.

Hebrews 4:12 NKJV

God's Word is alive and powerful; it's not dead; it's not lifeless; it's not powerless or weak; it's not ineffective.

When we speak the Word of God in faith, results will happen. It is as if Jesus Himself were speaking. We see how powerful His Words are from the very beginning in the book of Genesis when God said, 'Let there be light' and it was so. Those words He spoke created into existence what was nonexistent.

Jesus speaking in John 6:63 tells us that it is the Spirit that quickens (makes alive or gives life); the flesh profits nothing. The words that Jesus spoke were spirit and life. When we speak by the Spirit of God, it will be the same with us – it will produce life!

When we speak God's Word it has power. We are either speaking words of life or words of death and we will eat the fruit of whichever one we are speaking (Proverbs 18:21). As a little girl, I heard a saying that goes like this, "Sticks and stones may break my bones, but words will never hurt me." That saying is a lie according to this scripture. We need to choose and speak our words carefully so they will produce life and not death.

What is it you need to see come alive and be powerful in your life? Take the Word of God and apply it to your situation. In faith, speak it out loud and declare what it says over your life. Do not waver or doubt and YOU WILL see salvation come forth. YOU WILL see the Word of God come alive with power to produce what you are believing for.

We need to renew our minds in the Word of God daily. Let Him show forth His mighty power in excellence and majesty by agreeing and speaking forth what He says, not what we think, see, or feel. Many times, we limit God from working in our lives by the words we are speaking because they are doubt and unbelief. They are not producing the results He has for us.

Remember, His Word is alive and powerful and will discern the thoughts and intents of our heart!

GOD'S WORDS ARE
SWEETER THAN HONEY

———————— ♡ ————————

How sweet are your words to my taste,
sweeter than honey to my mouth!

Psalm 119:103 NKJV

There are a few scriptures that describe God's Word as being sweeter than honey. And who doesn't love the taste of honey? Sweet and soothing as it goes down. Raw (untainted, pure) honey has benefits: It has a variety of nutrients, it is rich in antioxidants, and it heals wounds.

The Word of God is much like raw honey in that it is pure and untainted (Psalm 12:6, Proverbs 30:5). The Lord tells us in Psalm 34:8 to taste and see that He is good. When we eat and feast on God's Word, as it says in Jeremiah 15:16, it will be the joy and rejoicing of our heart. It will be life and health to our flesh (Proverbs 4:20-22).

GOD'S WORD is described as so many incredible things, and here are a few of them:

- It is pure

- It will be nourishment to your spirit, soul, and body
- It is a lamp to our feet and a light to our path
- It is truth
- It is profitable for teaching, reproof, correction, and training in righteousness
- It will cause us to grow spiritually
- It stands forever
- It will not return void, but it will carry out the purpose for which it is sent
- It will save (make sound) your soul (will, mind, and emotions) as you renew your mind in it
- It will produce results as you pray according to His will (and His will is in His Word)
- It will produce life, peace, and health
- It will cause faith to arise in your heart (faith comes by hearing the Word of God)
- It will impart understanding to you
- It will cause you to know the truth as you abide in His Word, and it will set you free
- It is a blueprint for a successful life
- It is a seed that you plant in your heart that will grow and produce powerful results

So, feast on His Word and let it bring nourishment, healing, and refreshment to you this day!

HE FIRST LOVED US SO WE CAN LOVE ONE ANOTHER

―――――――――― ♡ ――――――――――

Beloved, let us love one another, for love is of God; and everyone who loves is born of God and knows God. He who does not love does not know God, for God is love. In this the love of God was manifested toward us, that God has sent His only begotten Son into the world, that we might live through Him. In this is love, not that we loved God, but that He loved us and sent His Son to be the propitiation for our sins. Beloved, if God so loved us, we also ought to love one another.

1 John 4:7-11 NKJV

There are times we get caught up in loving God because of what He can do for us and how He can bless us. Our mindset should be that we love God because He first loved us by giving us His one and only Son, Jesus.

Because of His love for us, we can now walk in that agape love toward others (once we are born again). As we are being conformed to His image and His likeness, we can then be the hands, feet, and mouth of Jesus to

71

others in this lost world. We should be giving to them what God has given to us, His unconditional love. He so loved that He gave.

Are we taking advantage of every opportunity that comes our way to minister that agape love? God will place people across our path that we may be the only ones who will speak a word of truth to them, be kind to them, or share with them the hope we have in Christ.

God's love and plan for humanity is so incredible that we cannot even understand it with our minds. Why? Because our carnal minds are an enemy to God. We cannot come to God with our minds. If you are living according to the flesh, it means your mind is set on the things of the flesh. If you renew your mind in the Word of God and set it on the things above, it will produce life and peace in you. It is then you will start to get a revelation of His love for you that you in turn can give to others.

We have the Spirit of the living God on the inside of us. And where the Spirit of the Lord is, there is freedom; freedom to be what God has called us to be and freedom to do what God has called us to do.

We are empowered to love others because He first loved us!

HE SAVED US ACCORDING TO HIS MERCY

---------- ♡ ----------

*He saved us, not because of the righteous
things we had done, but because of His mercy.
He washed away our sins, giving us a new birth
and new life through the Holy Spirit.*

Titus 3:5 NLT

There is nothing we can do to earn salvation; it is the gift of God to us demonstrating His mercy and His unconditional love for us. No matter how righteous a person thinks they are, one's own righteousness is as filthy rags (Isaiah 64:6). It is by faith through grace we are saved and not of ourselves; it is the gift of God (Ephesians 2:8-9). There is no boasting on our part. No flesh will glory (or boast) in the presence of God.

Romans 5:8 ties in with this, "But God demonstrates (to show or prove) His own love toward us, in that while we were still sinners, Christ died for us. Verse 9 continues, "Much more then, having now been justified (just as though we had never sinned) by His blood, we shall be saved from wrath through Him." (KJV)

The plan of God for mankind is really beyond

anything that words can describe. The love the Father showed toward us in giving His one and only Son to pay the price for our salvation is truly an incredible act of love.

This is a life in which we can have *total* victory in *every* situation we will ever walk through from the time we are born again until we go to be with the Lord. Stop and think about that for a minute. Do you really believe that is possible? Well, it is. But we have a part to play which is to BELIEVE AND RECEIVE BY FAITH WHAT HE HAS ALREADY ACCOMPLISHED FOR US ON THE CROSS.

This is not to say there will never be challenges and hard times, because there will be. Psalm 34:19 tells us that many are the afflictions of the righteous, but the Lord will deliver us out of them all. That's a powerful promise.

We have an enemy, the devil, who comes to steal, kill, and destroy, but Jesus came that we might have life and life more abundantly (John 10:10). We don't have to fear the enemy, but we need to know that he does exist. Just as God has a plan for our lives, so does the enemy. We have been given the authority to declare that the enemy's plan is cancelled over our lives, our children, and grandchildren. We can declare that no weapon formed against us shall prosper, but we will prosper over every weapon that is formed against us (Isaiah 54:17). We can declare and decree that we will walk in the plan and destiny that God has for us and our family, and that we will finish the race that God has set before us!

If bad things have happened in your life, be assured that God is the only one that can turn what the enemy intended for evil into good. There is no religion on the face of the earth that can have that kind of success. The reason? Because this is not a religion. It is a relationship with the man, Jesus Christ. He willingly gave His life for mankind so that we could have an abundant life.

We need to be encouraged by this great and unconditional love of our heavenly Father. If He is for us, who can be against us? No one or nothing!

HEALING IS GOD'S WILL FOR YOU

--------- ♡ ---------

But He was wounded for our transgressions, He was bruised for our iniquities: the chastisement for our peace was upon Him, and by His stripes we are healed.

Isaiah 53:5 NKJV

So many people want to know what God's will is for their life. One thing for sure is He wants you well -- free from sickness and disease. In fact, Jesus paid for your healing over 2000 years ago when He went to the cross and took every sin, sickness, and disease upon Himself. Study Isaiah 53:5, 1 Peter 2:24, Matthew 10:7-8, Psalm 107:20, along with Psalm 103 just for starters. Also, look at Matthew, Mark, Luke, and John where Jesus healed them all – every time! He is the same yesterday, today, and forever – He never changes.

Religion (which is rooted in deception) will tell you that God may heal you sometimes and other times He won't; maybe He wants to teach you a lesson through your sickness; maybe it's just your burden to carry in life, or maybe you've done something wrong, and the Lord is punishing you for it. These are all lies from the pit of hell.

If sickness and disease are such a blessing and God has allowed it in your life, then a question that ought to be asked is, "Why are you going to the doctor to get rid of it?"

John 10:10 says the enemy comes to steal, kill, and destroy, but Jesus came that we might have life and life more abundantly. Having sickness and disease in your body is not an abundant life, and it is NEVER the will of God. This is not condemnation, but it is speaking the truth in love. I was so thankful to learn these truths. God ONLY has good for you. If it's not good, it's not God. Such a simple truth, yet so divisive even in the church among believers.

When a person gets a revelation of the true nature of God and how good He really is, then they can reject those lies they have believed, and repentance can come forth. Repentance is simply turning from those lies to believing the truth. It is a change of heart.

I would encourage you to take the Word of God and read it for yourself. Then be honest with yourself, and before God, on what you are reading. If you are struggling to believe this, ask Him to remove the veil over your heart that has you blinded to what He did for you. None of us would do what this man Jesus did, and thank God we don't have to. He paid an incomprehensible price by giving His life so you and I could walk in *total freedom* from everything the enemy has planned for our lives.

What an awesome plan of God!

HOW TO BE PRODUCTIVE
IN THE KINGDOM OF GOD

───────── ♡ ─────────

Our people must learn to do good by meeting the urgent needs of others; then they will not be unproductive.

Titus 3:14 NLT

Do you feel you are being unproductive in your walk with the Lord? Or maybe another question to ask is, do you want to be productive in your walk with the Lord? The Bible has the answer for everything we need to know.

Titus 3:14 is a verse I came across that I had never seen before in the NLT. It popped right off the page! I'm sure the reason it did is because I always want to be fruitful and productive in my walk with the Lord. I always want to make a difference in the lives of others. And one of the ways to be productive is by meeting the urgent needs, or necessities, of others. It goes right along with the verse in Acts 20:35 where it says, "It is more blessed to give than to receive." Which is so true!

When we get our focus off self and have a desire to help others, there will be nothing more satisfying or fulfilling. God will place people across our path, or we may know people who have pressing needs, and we will be the very ones He uses to supply or meet that need. It could be praying for someone who has pain in their body and needs healing to take place or meeting a financial need that someone has or even bringing hope to someone who is in despair. God will show you; He will put it in your spirit when, where, how, and to whom.

Every day there are these kinds of opportunities that will present themselves if we are sensitive to the Spirit of God and His leading. He will reveal to us how to meet those urgent needs. All God wants is a willing and obedient vessel to show His love and power to others. When this happens, be assured, you are being productive in His Kingdom!

IF YOU CONTINUE IN
THE WORD OF GOD

———————— ♡ ————————

*Then Jesus said to those Jews which believed
on Him, "If ye continue in my Word, then are ye
my disciples indeed; And ye shall know the truth,
and the truth shall make you free."*

John 8:31-32 KJV

Jesus was speaking to those who believed in Him, but they were religious and didn't believe they were in bondage and needed to be set free.

There may be believers in Christ that think since they have their ticket to heaven, now everything is fine. They go on in life doing their own thing not considering what the Lord would have them do. They have never been set free from things that have them bound and things that are hindering them from walking in victory the way God intended for them to walk.

As we can see in these scriptures, just because someone has believed in the Lord does not mean they are automatically free. Their spirit man is completely perfect just like Jesus', but the soul (mind, will, and emotions) has never been set free from bondages and wrong thinking. Others can say *God has started* the process of setting us free to the degree He has because we are continuing, or abiding, in the Word of God. But this walk is a process.

The qualifications for getting set free are clarified in these two verses in John 8:31-32.

There are times you may only hear it quoted, "The truth shall make you free." But verse 31 needs to be quoted along with verse 32, which says, "Then said Jesus to those Jews which believed on Him, if you continue in my Word, then are ye my disciples indeed; and ye shall know the truth, and the truth shall make you free." The word 'continue' means to abide; and to abide in something is to dwell, endure, remain in it.

A disciple is a learner, a pupil, or one who follows another's teachings. According to this scripture, a disciple is one who continues or abides and dwells in the teachings of Jesus.

To know the truth is to be aware, perceive, and understand it. Jesus said in John 17:17, "Sanctify them through thy truth: thy Word is truth." John 1:17 tells us the law came by Moses, but *grace and truth* came by Jesus Christ.

Simply put, if we abide or remain in the Word of God, we are His disciples, His followers. It is then we shall know the truth of His Word and the truth of His Word will set us free. The more you renew your mind in the Word of God, the more truth you will be aware of, and understanding and revelation will come forth. The Word will set your thinking right, it will set your actions right, it will restore your soul, it will set your life on a path that is pleasing to God. It will set you *free from* bondages, lies, addictions, religion, and every hindrance that keeps you from walking in victory.

I would encourage you to continue in the Word of God and let patience (endurance, perseverance) have its perfect work in you so that you may be perfect and complete lacking nothing (James 1:4)!

JESUS HEALED ALL THAT WERE OPPRESSED

———— ♡ ————

And you know that God anointed Jesus of Nazareth with the Holy Spirit and with power. Then Jesus went around doing good and healing all who were oppressed by the devil, for God was with Him.

Acts 10:38 NLT

The word 'power' in this verse is the word dunamis and it means ability, might, strength, miraculous power. The anointing is placed on the inside of us for a purpose, just as it was in Jesus, to demonstrate the power of God to others. The anointing will always be to do good, as it says here in Acts 10:38.

If you are oppressed of the devil, God wants to set you free. Fear and oppression go hand in hand according to Isaiah 54:14, "In righteousness shalt thou be established: thou shalt be far from oppression; for thou shalt not fear; and from terror; for it shall not come near thee." (KJV)

Let's look at a few more words in our key scripture:

Went about - to traverse, come, depart, go abroad, over, travel, walk through

Doing good - to bestow a benefit, to do good

Healing - to make whole, to cure

All - all, any, every, whosoever

Oppressed - to exercise dominion against, to exercise power over

We could say it like this: Jesus traveled about bestowing benefits, curing everyone the devil was exercising dominion over and against.

People in the world are so oppressed by the devil and don't even know it. They don't know what to believe, who to believe, if they should believe, or even how to believe what they should be believing. And the devil is using all the evil going on in our world today to confuse and put people in fear. That is exactly what oppression will do to a person, and God wants to see them set free. This freedom comes by believing and receiving what Jesus paid for on the Cross.

The reason Jesus was able to demonstrate the power of God was because God was with Him, and He only did what the Father told Him to do (John 5:19). He never did His own thing, and we shouldn't either. We, as believers, have God with us and He says He will never leave us nor forsake us.

When we are about our Father's business, we can expect great and mighty things to take place. We can expect signs, wonders, miracles, and gifts of healing. We can expect the impossible to become possible because that is the God we serve - the God of the impossible.

Be ready to see God move in powerful ways showing His power in and through you to carry out His purposes in the earth to a hurting world. Let your light shine in this dark world. Be about your Father's business doing good and healing those who are oppressed of the devil.

John 14:12 tells us, "Verily, verily, I say unto you, He that believeth on me, the works that I do shall he do also; and greater works than these shall he do; because I go unto my Father." (KJV)

KEEP YOUR EYES ON JESUS

—————————— ♡ ——————————

Matthew 14:22-36

I love it when the Lord fixes your eyes on certain scriptures that pop off the pages of the Bible. This is what happened to me as I was reading in Matthew 14.

After Jesus had fed five thousand men, besides women and children, it says He constrained His disciples to get into a ship and go to the other side while He sent the multitudes away. Then He went alone to pray. While He was praying, there arose a storm out in the sea where the disciples were. It says the waves were tossing and the wind was contrary.

Jesus went out to the disciples walking on the water. They didn't recognize Him but thought He was a spirit, and they were troubled. They cried out in fear. Immediately Jesus spoke to them telling them to be of good cheer, or take courage, that it was Him and not to be afraid.

Matthew 14:28-30 in the KJV says, "And Peter answered him and said, Lord, if it be thou, bid me come unto thee on the water. And he said, "Come." And when Peter was come down out of the ship, he walked on the water, to go to Jesus. But when he saw the boisterous (violent) wind, he was afraid; and beginning to sink, he cried, saying, "Lord, save me." Of course, Jesus at once stretched forth His hand and caught him.

Jesus had given Peter a word and that was 'come'. But the storm (the enemy) going on around Peter caused him to doubt and get in fear instead of keeping his eyes fixed on Jesus and what He had told him. He focused on what was going on around him and began to sink.

In verse 31, when Jesus reached out to catch Peter, He told him he was of little faith and asked him why he doubted. When he got in the boat, the wind ceased. Then they worshipped Jesus and realized He was the Son of God.

What storm are you facing right now? Is there something the Lord has spoken to you, but while believing that word, a storm has brewed? Have you taken your eyes off the Lord and focused on the storm instead? Don't let the storms of life hinder your blessings by getting your focus off what God has told you.

The enemy always tries to create chaos right before a breakthrough. If we yield to that chaos, we are yielding to fear, doubt, and unbelief. This stops the power of God from coming forth with our victory.

As you read the rest of this chapter, there was something I noticed. Something great was about to happen, and the enemy, no doubt, didn't want it to take place.

It says Jesus and the disciples came to the land

of Gennesaret and when the men of that place recognized it was Jesus, they brought to Him ALL that were diseased. And as many as touched the hem of His garment were made perfectly whole, or well.

The enemy was wanting to stop the healing power of God from manifesting to those who were sick and diseased in Gennesaret by creating a storm. The enemy did not want those people free from pain and torment. Why? Because he is the author of pain and torment, sickness, and disease.

When the storms of life come our way, the enemy is wanting to get our eyes on the storm and off Jesus. The Lord is saying, "Turn your eyes back on Me and what I have said to you, not what is going on around you. As you do this, watch the storm cease and see the mighty power of God at work!"

LEAVING THE PAST BEHIND

———————— ♡ ————————

*Brethren, I do not count myself to have appre-
hended; but one thing I do, forgetting those
things which are behind and reaching forward
to those things which are ahead, I press toward
the goal for the prize of the upward call of God
in Christ Jesus.*

Philippians 3:13-14 NKJV

How many of you today are stuck in the past? Maybe
it's past regrets, past disappointments, or even past
failures. It could possibly be things in the past that
were good such as past achievements or accomplish-
ments that you didn't want to leave behind, but God
has something better ahead for you. He never intended
us to live in the past.

Paul was a great example of someone who chose
to forget (leave behind) the things that were behind
and press forward to what was ahead. God had a plan
for him from his mother's womb. Read Galatians 1 and
Acts 9. He was a chosen vessel to bring Jesus to the
Gentiles, kings, and the children of Israel. Yet, before
his conversion, he did terrible things by persecuting

Christians even some to the point of death. Had Paul not left those things behind, he never would have become the man God had chosen him to be to do the things He had chosen him to do in the Kingdom of God. But Paul made a *choice to go forward*. Only God can turn what the enemy intended for evil around for our good. He is the Restorer of Life and the Redeemer of Time. Read Joel 2:25. He is even the Repairer of the Breach (Isaiah 58).

An example at the other end of the spectrum is those who *chose to stay in the past*. You can read in the books of Exodus, Numbers and Deuteronomy about the Israelites, the children in the wilderness. God had a plan to bring them into the promised land of Canaan. It was described as a land flowing with milk and honey. They continually rebelled and murmured against their leaders, Moses and Aaron, but really it was against God (Exodus 16 and Numbers 14). It became so bad that they said they had it better in Egypt (as slaves) than in the wilderness. *In their hearts*, they turned back to Egypt.

You might have left physically where you want to be, but in your heart, you are holding on to the past. This will hinder what God has for you. All but two of them (Joshua and Caleb) died in the wilderness, because in their hearts they turned back and never entered the promised land that God had set before them. It says Joshua and Caleb had a different spirit about them and they entered the promised land.

Another example is Lot's wife. She looked back because she could not detach herself from the past (instead of going forward) and she became a pillar of salt (Genesis 19:26).

There is a time to deal with your past, but don't get stuck there. God has so much more ahead for you. Accept and receive God's forgiveness for whatever it is you are holding on to concerning the past. Today, move forward to the good He has prepared ahead for you!

LIFE IS IN THE BLOOD

———————— ♡ ————————

*For the life of the flesh is in the blood, and
I have given it to you upon the altar to make
atonement for your souls; for it is the blood that
makes atonement for the soul.*

Leviticus 17:11 NKJV

Just as in the natural realm, without blood in a body, that person is dead; so it is spiritually. Without the blood of Jesus, we are spiritually dead and without hope.

To really get an appreciation for what Jesus did by shedding His blood for us, let's first see what happened under the law of Moses, under the old covenant.

In Hebrews 9, beginning in verse 7, it tells us that the high priest went into the Holy of Holies to offer the blood of bulls and goats for the remission of people's sins. However, this never permanently removed the curse of sin. Once a year this had to be done. As it says in Hebrews 7:19, the law made nothing perfect, but the bringing in of a better hope did; by which we draw near unto God. Jesus was made a surety (guarantee) of a better covenant (verse 22) with better promises

(Hebrews 8:6).

God made Jesus our High Priest, and He offered Himself without spot to God by shedding His own blood to take away our sins once and for all. Once we believe in Him through faith, and we confess our sins, He is faithful and just to forgive us and cleanse us from all unrighteousness (1 John 1:9). It also says in Hebrews 9:14 that the blood of Jesus will purge (make clean) our conscience from dead works to serve the living God. This was God's plan from the beginning.

We do not have a high priest that cannot be touched (have compassion, sympathy) with the feelings of our infirmities (weaknesses, frailty, sicknesses, diseases); but was in ALL points tempted like we are, yet without sin. Because of that, we can come boldly to the throne of grace. We can obtain mercy and find grace to help in our time of need. We can come any time to the throne of grace through faith in His blood. The blood of Jesus is what gives us life in the Spirit.

On the cross there was an exchange made. Jesus, who knew no sin, became sin for us by going to the cross and shedding His blood, so that we might be made the righteousness of God in Him (2 Corinthians 5:21). We are cleansed, forgiven, justified (just as though we had never sinned), sanctified (set apart to God), redeemed, healed, protected and so much more by the blood of Jesus. It's hard to even fathom the kind of love and sacrifice that Jesus showed on the cross for you and me.

This precious gift of the blood of Jesus is where life is truly found!

LIGHT OVERCOMES DARKNESS

———————— ♡ ————————

The light shines in the darkness, and the darkness can never extinguish it.

John 1:5 NLT

Think of a dark room and what happens when you turn the light switch on. All that darkness is dispelled. Darkness cannot stay in the presence of light. So it is when you ask Jesus to come live on the inside of you. All the darkness that you once walked in will be expelled by the light of God as you begin to walk in His Word. It is a process. As you renew your mind in the Word of God, the light of the glorious gospel will begin shining in your heart and in your life more and more.

God wants to deliver you from the darkness that has you bound. If there are addictions, fear, depression, suicidal thoughts, mental anguish, hatred, anger or any other dark spirit that controls your life, come to Jesus and let His light shine on that darkness and set you free today.

There are only two kingdoms in this world – the kingdom of darkness and the Kingdom of light. People are either in one or the other. God wants to open people's eyes to turn them from darkness to light, from the power of Satan to God. There is no middle ground.

John 8:12 says in the NKJV, "Then Jesus spoke to them again, saying, "I am the light of the world. He who follows Me shall not walk in darkness but have the light of life." When you ask Jesus to come live on the inside of you and start following Him, you start walking in His light and in His life. You will be salt and light to the world and your light will not be hidden from those in darkness.

As it says in 1 John 1:7, "But if we walk in the light, as He is in the light, we have fellowship one with another, and the blood of Jesus Christ his Son cleanseth us from all sin." (KJV)

God is faithful, and the work He begins in a person, He will finish it. Allow Him to do His work of righteousness in you today!

LOVE NEVER FAILS

———— ♡ ————

Love never fails.

1 Corinthians 13:8 NKJV

Do you realize that if you walk in love (the love of God), you will never fail because love never fails? That's a guarantee because God doesn't lie, and His Word doesn't lie.

In the world, people are afraid of failing in their jobs, in their relationships, in raising their kids, in providing for their families, how they've invested their money, among other things. The truth is that fear is what allows the enemy to cause you to fail. Walking in God's love will cast out all fear (1 John 4:18), and it will cause you to succeed in all that you set your hand to do.

1 John 4:7-8 says, "Beloved, let us love one another: for love is of God; and everyone who loves is born of God and knows God. He who does not love does not love God, for God is love." (NKJV)

The love chapter, as it is known, is 1 Corinthians 13. This chapter shows us the very nature of God. This is the nature that is on the inside of us, in our born again spirit man.

Love suffers long (is patient, forbearing) and is kind; love does not envy, love does not parade itself; is not puffed up (not in pride), does not behave rudely, does not seek its own, is not provoked, thinks no evil; does not rejoice in iniquity, but rejoices in the truth (the Word), bears all things, believes all things, hopes all things, endures all things. Love never fails.

God is love. Love will never leave us nor forsake us; Love will always protect us; Love will cause us to prosper in every area of our lives; Love will cover a multitude of sins.

When we get a revelation of God's love, and that it never fails and is always for us, we will have a revelation of what success in the Spirit truly is!

MOVED WITH COMPASSION

───────── ♡ ─────────

He who says he abides in Him ought himself
also to walk just as He walked.

1 John 2:6 NKJV

Many years back, I did a study on compassion. I looked up scriptures throughout Matthew, Mark, Luke, and John where Jesus showed, or was moved with, compassion (pity) towards people. He is our example of how we should be walking. Like our key verse says, if we say we abide in Him, we ought to walk even as He walked.

These are some things I saw when Jesus was moved with compassion:

He healed those that were sick and diseased; He delivered those who had demons; He fed the crowds by multiplying the loaves and fish; He raised the dead (one example being the young man who died, who was the only son of his mother. Jesus saw her weeping and had compassion on her and raised the son from the dead and gave him back to his mother); He came upon a crowd and saw they were sheep without a shepherd, and He taught them many things; He would go after the one that was lost and leave the ninety-nine that had not gone astray.

Compassion will put the needs of others above one's own feelings and desires. Let's look at Mark 6:31, which shows this example.

Jesus sent the twelve apostles out two by two to cast out devils and heal the sick. When the disciples returned from ministering, Jesus saw they were tired. He said to them, "Let's go off by ourselves to a quiet place and rest awhile." There were so many people coming to them that *they didn't even have time to eat*. They got in a boat and headed to a place *where they could be by themselves to rest*. When the people saw them leaving, they went on ahead of them to where they would be. It says that Jesus stepped out of the boat and had *compassion* on them because they were as sheep without a shepherd. And he taught them there. The apostle's needs and desires (for rest and food) did not stop Jesus from showing His compassion to the crowd of people. This is where He then multiplied the loaves and fish, and they all ate and were filled.

When we put aside our own desires, which may be an inconvenience at the time, and do the Father's will in showing compassion, miracles will happen. This is a demonstration of the love of God for people. This is where our hearts should be -- desiring to show the compassion and love of God even over our own plans and schedules. It is getting 'self' out of the way and being 'Christ-centered'!

NOT ME, BUT GOD'S GRACE WITHIN ME

———— ♡ ————

For I am the least of the apostles, that am not meet (worthy) to be called an apostle, because I persecuted the church of God. But by the grace of God I am what I am: and His grace which was bestowed upon me was not in vain; but I laboured more abundantly than they all: yet not I, but the grace of God which was with me.

1 Corinthians 15:9-10 KJV

Saul, before his name was changed to Paul, persecuted the Church and had Christian men and women committed to prison and even killed. On the road to Damascus, he had an encounter with the Lord and was blinded for three days, which you can read about in Acts 9.

Jesus says in Acts 9:15 that Saul was a chosen vessel to bear His name before the Gentiles, and kings, and children of Israel. As deceived as Saul was, God had chosen him from the beginning for a specific purpose to bring the gospel to the Gentiles to testify of Jesus and His resurrection from the dead. That was the grace of God upon him, and that grace was not in vain, or empty. Paul toiled more than any of them, yet it was not him, but God's grace that was with him. He knew God had done some profound things in his life, and he took no credit for it.

God has a plan and purpose for all our lives as well (Jeremiah 29:11). Likewise, so does the devil, just like he did with Saul prior to his encounter on the road to Damascus. You may be saying, "Well, I've done too many bad things where God couldn't use me." The truth is, God never uses perfect people, which we just saw in this example. Like many other people in the Bible that you can read about, you will see the same thing. They were not perfect, yet God had a call on their lives. It simply takes a humble heart to receive and walk in the calling that God places upon you. It will be His grace working in you to fulfill the plan He has chosen for you.

If you could fulfill the calling of God with your own abilities and qualifications, you wouldn't need God. He doesn't call the qualified; He qualifies those He calls and then He gets all the glory out of what He does in and through you and me, just like in Paul's life.

Let the grace of God do His mighty work in and through your life for His glory so that we can say as Paul said, "By the grace of God I am what I am!"

NOTHING CAN CHANGE
GOD'S LOVE FOR YOU

———————— ♡ ————————

But God demonstrates His own love toward us, in that while we were still sinners, Christ died for us.

Roman 5:8 NKJV

It doesn't matter how many times you try to do things to please God (i.e., read more, pray more, give more), your self-effort will not get Him to love you more. And no matter how much you have messed up and gone off the deep end, God will not love you any less. While we were yet sinners, God proved His unconditional love for us. There are absolutely no conditions to get Him to love you more or love you less. God's love towards us is not performance based - period! It is pure love like no other.

People who have messed up and think that there is no way God could love them is because they are seeing God through the filter of their own soul (mind, will, and emotions). The other end of the spectrum is self-righteousness, which is of the law. They think their good works and good behavior will get God to approve of them and love them more. Both spectrums are deception. They are both based in religion, which is living under the law and not grace (Romans 6:14).

God loved the world in the sinful state we were in. It is not that God approves of sin, He doesn't. But He loves us and has a plan for us to believe on Him so that He can change our lives from darkness to light from the power of Satan to the power of God (Acts 26:18).

If you are having a struggle today believing the love of God, ask Him to reveal Himself to you. Ask Him to give you a revelation of His love for you which He proved when He gave His Son Jesus to die, be buried, and be raised from the dead. He did this not only so you can spend eternity in heaven with Him forever, but so you can have a personal relationship with the man, Jesus, and experience heaven on earth. It tells us in John 17:3 that eternal life is to know the one and only true God and Jesus His Son whom He sent.

What a blessing to know Him and the power of His resurrection by walking in His unconditional love!

PLANTING SEED IN YOUR HEART

—————— ♡ ——————

Matthew 13, Mark 4, Luke 8

This parable is recorded in these three books of the Bible. It talks about planting the seed (God's Word) in the soil or ground (of our heart) to bring forth a harvest. Just as in the natural realm when you plant a seed nto the ground, depending on the type of soil, among other things, that will determine the harvest you get from that seed.

There are four types of soil mentioned in this parable, and it is showing the four different types of the heart of man. When we hear the Word of God, our hearts are considered one of these four types of ground.

The first one is considered the wayside heart. This is where the Word is sown but Satan comes immediately and takes away the Word sown in their hearts because they don't understand it unless they should believe and be saved. The rocky, or stony heart, which is the second one, is where they hear the Word and immediately receive it with gladness or joy, yet they have no root in themselves, so they only endure for a time. Afterward, when persecution or tribulation comes for the Word's sake, they are immediately offended and stumble. The third heart which is the thorny heart is the heart that hears the Word, but the cares of the world, the deceitfulness of riches, and the lust for other things enter in and choke the Word and it becomes unfruitful. The one that produces a thirty, sixty, or one hundred-fold (harvest) is the fourth type of heart, which is the honest and good heart, which hears the Word and keeps it and bears fruit. As we begin to grow in the Lord by hearing, receiving, understanding, and keeping His Word, we should eventually come to the place of an honest and good heart.

I would encourage you today to read this parable in the three different books listed above and ask God for understanding of this parable so that you can start seeing the Word of God produce fruit in your life. Jesus said if we don't understand this parable, how will we understand any of the other ones? We won't.

As you plant the seed of the Word in your heart, the Word will start producing what you need in your life. Even while you sleep, it will start working as it says in Mark 4:26-27. It will be an effortless change that takes place on the inside of you!

PLEASE GOD – NOT MAN

———————— ♡ ————————

But as we have been approved by God to be entrusted with the gospel, even so we speak, not as pleasing men, but God who tests our hearts.

1 Thessalonians 2:4 NKJV

Did you know if you're pleasing God, it doesn't matter what people think or say? That should take all the pressure off you trying to please a man. Paul made it clear in Galatians 1:10 that if we are looking to please men, or win approval of men, we are not the servants of Christ. That's a humbling statement! There are people who will do anything to please another person, even at the cost of their job, or their reputation, or their relationships. Who are we looking to please?

When we are preaching the gospel, we won't be using flattering words or seeking glory from men. We will only want to be pleasing God by doing His will from the heart. In John 5:44, Jesus tells us that when we receive honor from one another and are not seeking the honor that comes from *God only*, we are not believing.

If you choose to please God, you will please some

men. But ultimately, it doesn't matter if you have man's approval or not. God is the only one you should ever try to please because He will reward you far above what man can do for you (Hebrews 11:6). He alone is the one who tries, or examines, the heart of man. He doesn't look on the outward appearance of a person like man does. God looks on the heart of man. He sees beyond what a man sees in another person. And He is the one who will exalt and promote you.

It is an honor to have God approve us and entrust us with this gospel. It is something we should not take lightly. I will take God's approval any day over what man thinks!

REJOICE, PRAY, AND GIVE THANKS

---------- ♡ ----------

Rejoice evermore. Pray without ceasing. In everything give thanks: for this is the will of God in Christ Jesus concerning you.

1 Thessalonians 5:16-18 KJV

Are you wanting to know what God's will is for your life? If so, these 3 simple statements may be the very answer you need. They are easy to do when things are going well, but the true test is when everything is falling apart around you. Then it may not be so easy, until you overcome your flesh. Many times, this is when we yield to self-pity or murmuring and complaining.

I love what is says in Habakkuk 3:17-19. Verse 17 tells us that nothing was going well with Habakkuk, but he said in verse 18-19 (KJV), "Yet I will rejoice in the Lord, I will joy in the God of my salvation. The Lord God is my strength, and He will make my feet like hind's feet, and He will make me to walk upon mine high places." Habakkuk's confidence and trust was in God.

It takes a disciplined will to do what the Word of God says over how we feel in our flesh. It takes a determination to apply the instructions He gives us when we would rather do just the opposite. If we will choose to *do* the will of God, we will see victory. When we choose to be a *doer* of His Word, and not just a hearer only, we won't be deceived (James 1:22).

Philippians 4:4 says in the NKJV, "Rejoice in the Lord always. Again I will say, rejoice!" This shows we don't just rejoice when things are only good, but always; even when things may be at their worst.

The word 'rejoice' means to be calmly happy, joyful, glad, and cheerful. It will turn what might look hopeless into a radical change for good that otherwise might not come forth. This makes no sense to our natural (carnal) mind, and it never will. Our natural mind is an enemy to God as it tells us in Romans 8:7. But if we are spiritually minded it is life and peace (verse 6).

Today, decide in your heart that you will rejoice in the Lord, that you will pray, and that you will give Him thanks. The Word always works when we apply it!

RESTORATION OF HEALTH

———————— ♡ ————————

For I will restore health to you and heal you of your wounds, says the Lord, because they called you an outcast saying: This is Zion; No one seeks her.

Jeremiah 30:17 NKJV

Did you know this was carried out when Jesus went to the cross and shed His blood for you and me? He paid the price for every sickness, every disease, and every wound that would be inflicted on you and me when He said, "It is finished."

You may be asking, "Well, why am I still sick and why do I still have so many wounds and bruises on the inside of me?" The answer is because we have a part to play! Grace (Jesus) has already done His part, but Faith (us) must believe and receive what Grace has already provided.

To restore means to bring something back to its original condition; to repair or renovate. Think about people who restore homes or cars to their original, or previous, condition. This is what God wants to do in your life. He wants you restored to how He created man in the beginning before the fall in the garden - which is whole, sound, complete, nothing missing, nothing lacking in your life.

Before the fall of man in the garden, everything was perfect, complete. But when Adam and Eve sinned, the earth came under a curse and that is why Jesus came and did what He did for humanity, so that we could be restored back to how it was in the garden before the fall of man. That is exciting news!

In Genesis 1:26-27, God said, "Let Us make man in Our image, according to Our likeness; let them have dominion over the fish of the sea, over the birds of the air, over the cattle, over the earth and over every creeping thing that creeps on the earth. So, God created man in his own image; in the image of God, He created him; male and female He created them." (NKJV)

It doesn't matter what sickness or disease you may have in your body or what wounds, hurts, or bruises are on the inside of you, Jesus paid for it with His blood. You may be in a hospital room right now with no hope because of an incurable diagnosis. If you will believe these words and receive by faith that you are healed by the stripes of Jesus, you can experience total healing in your body. God is saying to you, "Rise and be healed."

When you are in faith declaring the truth of God's Word, the manifestation of what you are believing for has no choice but to come forth. If it takes having to speak the truth of God's Word every day all throughout the day, rather than go by what you feel or see, then do it. Breakthrough will come.

Persistence is what it takes, especially if you've had something or gone through something for a long time. We must persevere in prayer and use the authority God has given us over the enemy and all his attacks. The enemy knows when we mean business, and he will bow if we don't lose heart and cave in. It tells us in James 4:7 to submit ourselves to God, resist the devil and he will flee from us. Praise God!

It says in Luke 10:19 in the NKJV, "Behold, I give *YOU* the authority to trample on serpents and scorpions, and over *all* the power of the enemy, and nothing shall by any means hurt you." We have been given power and authority over the enemy and all his plans and schemes for our life.

You may have wounds festering on the inside of you. You may have hurts from the past, disappointments from people, or regrets. We have the authority in the name of Jesus to cancel every plan he has devised for our life – including sickness, disease, hurts, and wounds.

As you speak and declare these truths, God's power will work in you to deliver you. Psalm 147:3 says He heals the brokenhearted and binds up (heals) their wounds. There may even be people you need to forgive that have hurt or wounded you. Unforgiveness will keep these things festering inside of you, which eventually will come out of you in ways that can do harm.

You can cancel the enemy's plan over your life and release God's plan and goodness over yourself. Speak it out loud in faith – declare what Jesus did for you on the cross. Any and every little bit of progress you see, give God thanks for it. Expect more to come until you have put these hindrances and bondages completely out of your life.

The price has been paid – so believe and receive it just like you would if someone gave you a gift. You wouldn't just let that gift sit there. You would take it - receive it, open it, and put it to use knowing it's yours. This is no different with the Word of God; take what rightfully belongs to you as a gift from Jesus.

Remember, Jesus has already paid the price for whatever it is you are needing to overcome. And the victory that overcomes is *YOUR* faith!

SEEK FIRST

───────── ♡ ─────────

But seek first the kingdom of God and His righteousness, and all these things shall be added to you.

Matthew 6:33 NKJV

What are you seeking *first* in your life? Is it a relationship? Is it your job? Is it money? Is it a hobby? Is it possessions such as houses and cars?

Many people seek 'things' first and then are left unfulfilled, unsatisfied, and lacking purpose in life. The reason being, things can never satisfy us for long, only God can! Psalm 107:9 says He will satisfy the longing soul and fill the hungry soul with good *things*.

To seek the Kingdom of God is to seek the King's dominion and His way. To learn about the Kingdom, we need to get into the Owner's manual (the Word of God) and learn how the Owner operates it. It is a blueprint for our lives.

The world has one way of doing things and that is through painful toil and sweat which produces worry, fear, and stress. But God's Kingdom and His righteousness produces peace and calmness and a quietness and assurance forever – Isaiah 32:17. Which had you rather have?

We have all heard that some of the richest people in the world are the most miserable people. This shows that money cannot buy happiness and joy. There is a God given vacuum in each of us that *only* He can fill and satisfy. The issue is not about how much money or things we can accumulate, but it is about how God created man to have fellowship and relationship with Him. Only then can that satisfy the longing soul that money and things cannot fill. Remember though, it's the 'love' of money that is the root of all evil – not money. Money is just a tool for us to use.

It tells us in Matthew 6:24 that you cannot serve two masters. You will either hate one and love the other; or you will hold on to one and despise the other. You cannot serve God and money. God delights to give us all these things. But there is a prerequisite for obtaining them His way, and that is seeking *first* the Kingdom of God and His righteousness.

We are not to take thought, or worry, about what we eat, how we are clothed, or where we will live. God is saying that when we put Him first, He will *add* every one of these things to us. And He will always do exceedingly, abundantly above all we ask or think because of His power that works in us (Ephesians 3:20).

God's blessings will always exceed our own!

STAY THE COURSE

———————— ♡ ————————

I have fought a good fight, I have finished my course, I have kept the faith:

2 Timothy 4:7 KJV

God wants each one of us to finish our course (our race) and finish it in faith.

You may be going through a season where nothing seems to be working -- still unanswered prayers and promises; nothing in the physical looks like it's changing....... BUT GOD!! He is saying to stay the course and not quit or give up on Him because He hasn't given up on you.

It takes faith to keep believing when nothing seems to be working, or so you think it's not working. However, God is always working on your behalf behind the scenes. This is when you use your will to believe God and continue believing (staying with it) until you see the results of what you're believing for. Faith only considers what God says - not what it sees, feels, or thinks. This is where your faith will be tested and tried like gold being put through the fire. Then it comes out purified and refined. Faith also doesn't have a timeframe - it only keeps looking to Jesus knowing He is faithful to perform His promises. One day is as a thousand years and a thousand years is as one day to the Lord!

One example that is always so encouraging to me is Abraham. The promise God gave to him about a son came forth 25 years after God had spoken it to him. During all those years, his faith was being tested and tried until it was perfected to the point where there was no question *IF* God would bring it to pass, but he *KNEW* God would bring it to pass. And sure enough, it came to pass; his son of promise, Isaac, was born.

When God makes a promise to you, He is faithful to bring it to pass as long as you continue believing Him and stay the course. The closer it gets to the manifestation, your heart will be at a place that you know without a doubt it will be performed because you have taken all limits off God. You trust Him to align everything according to His perfect will. Much like a puzzle, all the pieces must fit together until that last piece is in place and the puzzle is then completed.

God is faithful and more than willing to bring to pass what He has spoken to you. But like the children of Israel who had been given a promise, they never saw it because of unbelief. If you know there is unbelief in your heart, be like the man that said, "Lord, I believe, help thou my unbelief." And do you know what? God will do just that. How do I know? He's done it for me.

Worship and praise Him and give Him thanks every day, knowing that He is working in you both to will and to do of His good pleasure (Philippians 2:13).

Stay in that place of rest because in that place of rest there is confidence and full assurance that what God has said, He will surely perform!

STRENGTH AND PEACE

———— ♡ ————

The Lord will give strength unto His people;
the Lord will bless His people with peace.

Psalm 29:11 KJV

Do you need strength and peace in your life today?

There is a certain time of year that always seems to put stress and pressure on people more than any other time – and that is Christmas. This seems to be a time of year when people get their focus off the Lord and on the care and busyness of the Christmas season. The good news? You don't have to allow it. You have a choice - yes, even during all that is going on in your world, you have a choice to say, "NO, I will not allow worry or stress to dictate my life, no matter what time of the year it is."

God wants to strengthen you and give you His peace when the stress and pressures of life knock at your door. Stop and pause and give Him thanks for who He is and for every blessing He has given you. Maybe write things down that He has done for you that you're thankful for.

He wants you free from all the cares that weigh you down, all the distractions that are right in front of you that allow worry and anxiety to rule in your heart. Don't let the enemy steal God's peace out of your heart. Instead, let God's peace rule over whatever it is the enemy is trying to steal from you. Rejoice in this day that the Lord has made and be glad in it.

In Isaiah 32:17-18 (NKJV) it tells us, "The work of righteousness will be peace, and the effect of righteousness, quietness and assurance forever. My people will dwell in a peaceable habitation, in secure (safe) dwellings and in quiet resting places..." I love His peace and quietness. My life did not always have that until I let His work of righteousness have its way in my heart.

If you are not seeing this peace and quietness in your life, there's no condemnation. Just know, you are not letting God's righteousness do a work of peace on the inside of you. Oppression, stress, fear, and whatever else is weighing you down, can lift off in a split second as you turn your heart back onto the Lord. He will strengthen you, and He will bless you with HIS peace.

Know He loves you and will never leave you nor forsake you. So, rest in this promise today!

THE EARTH FILLED WITH THE KNOWLEDGE OF GOD

──────── ♡ ────────

For the earth will be filled with the knowledge
of the glory of the Lord, as the waters cover the
sea.

Habakkuk 2:14 NJKV

In this chapter, the prophet Habakkuk sees a vision. He waits to see what the Lord says to him. Then he asks Him some questions concerning the vision.

In Habakkuk 2:2-3, the Lord said, "Write the vision, and make it plain upon tables, that he may run that readeth it. For the vision is yet for an appointed time, but at the end it shall speak, and not lie: though it tarry, wait for it; because it will surely come, it will not tarry." (KJV)

It then talks about how the just shall live by His faith. You might read this chapter, or better yet all 3 chapters in Habakkuk.

Verse 14 continues:

For the earth will be *filled*: to be full of; to accomplish; to flow with

With the *knowledge* of: the knowing; the acknowledging or awareness of

The *glory* of the Lord: the splendor; the honor; the weight (in a good sense); copiousness (fullness or abundant supply)

As the waters *cover* the sea: conceal, hide, overwhelm

When the earth is filled with the knowledge of the Lord's glory, every man, woman, and child will know there is a God in heaven who is full of majesty, honor, glory and power. The greatness, powerfulness, splendor, and goodness of God will be known throughout the whole earth.

Verse 20 ends with, ""But the Lord is in His holy temple: let all the earth keep silence before Him." (KJV)

Even the evildoers will be silenced at the awesomeness of God and His glory!

THE EYES OF THE LORD
ARE ON THE RIGHTEOUS

———————— ♡ ————————

The eyes of the Lord are on the righteous,
and His ears are open to their cry.

Psalm 34:15 NJKV

Do you ever feel like your prayers are going up to the ceiling and stopping there? Do you want the Lord to hear your prayers, and not only hear them, but answer them?

First, you need to know that you are *righteous* in Him. This is not your own righteousness, which is based on your performance, which is self-righteousness, which is of the law. But it is the righteousness of God inside of your born again spirit man. God made Jesus to be sin for us, who knew no sin; that we might be made the righteousness of God in Him (2 Corinthians 5:21).

When we know who we are in Christ, which is righteous by faith, then His eyes and ears are open to our prayers. If we are praying according to the will of God (which is key), it says in 1 John 5:14 that we can have confidence (boldness) that if we ask anything according to His will, He hears us. But it doesn't stop there. It goes on in verse 15 saying that if we know (are confident) He hears us, whatsoever we ask, we know that we have the petitions that we asked of Him. Notice it says *we have* the petitions - not maybe will get them, but *we have* them. It's a done deal! Faith receives the answer before it sees it.

The effectual fervent (active, mighty) prayer of the righteous man is what avails much (James 5:16). This type of prayer is powerful and produces great results. It also tells us in Proverbs that the prayer of the righteous shall be granted and the prayer of the upright is His delight. When you know you are righteous by faith, your prayers will get mighty results because they will get the attention of God because His eyes are on you!

Again, the key to getting your prayers answered is knowing you are righteous in Him and praying according to HIS will and not your own!

THE EYES OF THE LORD
ARE SEARCHING

———— ♡ ————

*For the eyes of the Lord run to and fro through-
out the whole earth, to show Himself strong on
behalf of those whose heart is loyal to Him.*

2 Chronicles 16:9 NKJV

The Lord is looking to find people that He can show
Himself strong on their behalf. When our hearts are
found fully committed and devoted to Him, this will
take place.

- This is a heart whose focus is on seeking first
  the Kingdom of God and His righteousness and
  all things will be added unto him - Matthew 6:33
- This is a heart whose mind is stayed on the
  Lord and will be kept in perfect peace because
  they trust Him - Isaiah 26:3
- This is a heart who is not afraid of evil tidings
  because his heart is fixed and established in
  truth trusting in the Lord - Psalm 112:7-8
- This is a heart that sets their love upon the
  Lord, and they call upon Him and He answers

and delivers them and honors them with long life - Psalm 91:14-16

- This is a heart that forgets the past and reaches forth to things that are ahead so that he obtains the prize of the high calling of God in Christ Jesus - Philippians 3:13-14

- This is a heart that isn't anxious or worried about anything, but offers prayers and supplications with thanksgiving unto God, and the peace of God that surpasses all understanding will keep their hearts and minds through Christ Jesus - Philippians 4:6-7

- This is a heart that is not condemned and keeps God's Words and does what is pleasing to Him. This heart will have confidence towards God and can ask whatsoever it desires *according to His will* and will receive from Him those petitions - 1 John 3:21-22

- This is a heart that is guarded (protected) with all diligence because out of it flows the issues of life - Proverbs 4:23

Everything in the Kingdom of God flows from what is within our hearts. When our hearts get in alignment with the truth of God's Word, and we know how much He loves us, He will come through in mighty ways and shew Himself strong on our behalf. If God be for us, who can be against us? Nothing or no one!

THE FEAR OF THE LORD

———— ♡ ————

Let all the earth fear the Lord; let all the inhab-
itants of the world stand in awe of Him.

Psalm 33:8 ESV

A question we should ask ourselves is, "Do we fear the Lord? Are we in awe of Him?"

The word fear here means reverence or awe of God's holiness. When we fear the Lord, there will be respect for Him and for His authority in our lives. When we have the fear of the Lord, we will turn from the ways of the world and turn towards His ways. When we fear the Lord, we will not fear man or what man can do to us. Our trust will be in the Lord.

The Bible is full of scriptures on the fear of the Lord, so let's look at several and see what they say.

The fear of the Lord:

- Is clean (pure) and endures forever – Psalm 19:9
- His secret will be with you, and He will show you (cause you to know) His covenant – Psalm 25:14
- Will cause you to be blessed, your seed to be

mighty upon the earth, wealth and riches to be in your house when you are delighting greatly in His Words - Psalm 112:1-3

- Is the beginning of wisdom, knowledge, and understanding – Psalm 111:10, Proverbs 1:7, Proverbs 2:5, Proverbs 9:10
- Is the foundation of true wisdom – Psalm 111:10
- Is to depart from evil; and it will be health to your body and strength to your bones – Proverb 3:7-8
- Is to hate evil – Proverbs 8:13
- Is the instruction of wisdom – Proverbs 15:33
- Will cause you to be blessed, you will eat the fruit of your labor, and it will be well with you – Psalm 128
- Will prolong your days – Proverbs 10:27
- You will have strong confidence (be secure) and your children will have a place of refuge – Proverbs 14:26
- Is a fountain of life (a source or supply for an abundant life) – Proverbs 14:27
- It leads to life, and you shall abide satisfied and not be visited with evil – Proverbs 19:23
- Along with humility, it will produce riches, honor, and life – Proverbs 22:4
- Will cause it to be well with you and your children – Deuteronomy 5:29

When we truly fear the Lord, we will want to obey Him and conform to His image. We will trust Him and be assured of His goodness. Everything we need in this life will be supplied through Him.

In Isaiah 11:2, one of the seven spirits of the Lord is the fear of the Lord. Just as Jesus feared His Father, it was a good and positive kind of fear. He trusted His Father and submitted to the Father's will for Him – even to the point of death on the Cross. He trusted what the Father said to Him that on the third day He would be raised from the dead. Because of His obedience and reverence to the Father, He was highly exalted and given a name that is above every name.

Had Jesus not feared and obeyed the Father, where would we be today? The answer is without hope, without a Savior, and without eternal life. When we truly fear the Lord, we will be walking in the truths of the Word of God – obeying His will for our lives and seeing His blessings come upon us and overtake us (Deuteronomy 28:2).

It says in Isaiah 33:6 NLT, "In that day He will be your sure foundation, providing a rich store of salvation, wisdom, and knowledge. The fear of the Lord will be your treasure."

Think of what a treasure is. It is something of value and worth. It is something that is cherished and held in high esteem. When we fear the Lord and treasure Him and His Word, that is where our heart will be (Luke 12:34)!

THE KINGDOM OF GOD

———————— ♡ ————————

*For the Kingdom of God is not eating and
drinking, but righteousness and peace and joy
in the Holy Spirit. For he who serves Christ in
these things is acceptable to God and approved
by men.*

Romans 14:17-18 NJKV

Isn't it great to know that what we eat and drink is
not based on God's Kingdom, but His Kingdom is based
on righteousness, peace, and joy in the Holy Ghost?

Let's look at righteousness, peace, and joy:

The *righteousness* of God is by faith unto all and
upon all that will believe. It has nothing to do with
our own righteousness, which is self-righteousness.
Righteousness is the very character and nature of
God. And we are to awake (rouse ourselves out of a
stupor) to righteousness and sin not. In 2 Corinthians
5:21, it says that God made Jesus to be sin for us, who
knew no sin, that we might be made the righteousness
of God in Him. What an exchange – our sin for His
righteousness!

His *peace* (quietness and rest) is a peace that goes beyond human understanding. It is a peace that you can have right in the middle of the storm. We are to let His peace rule (to govern; act as an umpire) in our hearts (Colossians 3:15).

Joy is a fruit of the Spirit. It is a calm delight and gladness. It is not based on circumstances. We can let joy bubble up from our spirit because it says the joy of the Lord is our strength. You can draw from God's joy that is inside your born again spirit man to give you strength in your time of need. When joy is present, all your problems will seem like nothing. You may ask, "How can that be?" Because your focus will not be on your problems, but on the joy of the Lord. In His presence there is FULLNESS of joy and at His right hand there are pleasures forevermore (Psalm 16:11).

I love that it says that if we serve Christ in these three things (righteousness, peace, and joy), it is acceptable to God, and we will be approved by men. This is the Kingdom of God at work in a believer's life who will choose to let it work in and through them. We can't lose for winning in this walk with the Lord!

THE LORD IS GOOD

—————————— ♡ ——————————

For the Lord is good. His unfailing love continues forever, and His faithfulness continues to each generation.

Psalm 100:5 NLT

Our (fleshly) love will fail, but walking in the love of God will never fail, so we will never fail. If we are not seeing victory in every area of our lives, it's because of a lack of the revelation of the love of God towards us.

What area in your life today are you not seeing your faith produce victory? Faith only works through love. And the victory that overcomes the world (your problems) is your faith (which works through love).

I truly believe that any and every answer, or victory, we need in this life will come through a revelation of His love for us. It is the foundation of our walk with God. When we truly know how much He loves us, that He is for us and not against us, and because of what He provided on the Cross for us, we will gain victory over the enemy's plans every time. When we *believe* God's truth over his lies, truth always wins. It's a guarantee.

Here are a few truths about God's unconditional love for you:

- Nothing can separate you from the love of God – Romans 8:37-39
- Faith works through love, and without faith it is impossible to please Him – Galatians 5:6, Hebrews 11:6
- God's love casts out all fear – 1 John 4:18
- God's love is never tied to performance; you cannot earn His love – John 3:16
- God's love is perfected in you by keeping His Word and being a doer of the Word, not just a hearer only – 1 John 2:5, James 1:22
- Love never fails; faith, hope, love; the greatest of these is love – 1 Corinthians 13:8,13

Ask God today to give you a revelation, or deepen what revelation you do have, of His love towards you. He proved His love towards us by giving His one and only Son, Jesus, to die and be raised from the dead so we could walk in total victory in our lives.

God is faithful to His Word and to His promises. His Word will never return void, but it will carry out the purpose for which it's been sent. Expect breakthrough today in believing that God loves you and His love towards you is unconditional and without limits!

THE LORD OF THE BREAKTHROUGH

———————— ♡ ————————

*So David went to Baal Perazim, and David
defeated them there; and he said, The Lord has
broken through my enemies before me, like a
breakthrough of water. Therefore, he called the
name of that place Baal Perazim.*

2 Samuel 5:20 NKJV

In 2 Samuel 5:17-20, when the Philistines (enemies)
heard that David had been anointed king of Israel, they
went out to search for him and capture him. So, David
asked the Lord if he should go up against them and
would He deliver them into his (David's) hand? And
the Lord told him to go, and that yes, He would deliver
them, without doubt, into his hand.

Even though David's enemies were *people* opposing
him, what 'enemies' are you needing to breakthrough in
your life today? The God of the breakthrough is more
than ready to give you whatever victories you are needing today. It may be with people like it was with David.
Or it may be a physical breakthrough you need in your
body. It may be an emotional breakthrough, a relational

breakthrough, or even a financial breakthrough you need to see take place. It doesn't matter what it is, it was defeated and disarmed 2000 years ago when Jesus went to the Cross and rose from the dead.

The God of the breakthrough is here today to bring you through in total victory. Nothing is too hard for Him, and nothing is impossible for Him (Luke 1:37).

Just like David, you can see your enemies fall right in front of you. Jesus is the same yesterday, today, and forever; He never changes (Hebrews 13:8).

Once at a home fellowship group, as we were praying, the Lord showed me that there were big breakthroughs coming. I saw in the Spirit a gate, and as that gate was opened, the water broke through like a flood. Afterward, as I looked up the word 'breakthrough' in the Bible, the Lord led me to these scriptures. It was encouraging, to say the least. Breakthrough came forth!

So, whatever enemies are opposing you, whether it be your family, your boss, your body, your finances, people at your work, expect the God of the Breakthrough to breakthrough like a flood in total victory!

THE NAME ABOVE ALL NAMES

———————— ♡ ————————

Therefore God also has highly exalted Him and given Him the name which is above every name, that at the name of Jesus every knee should bow, of those in heaven, and of those on earth, and of those under the earth, and that every tongue should confess that Jesus Christ is Lord, to the glory of God the Father.

Philippians 2:9-11 NKJV

In Philippians 2, it tells us that because Jesus humbled Himself and became obedient to death, the death of the cross, God highly exalted Him and gave Him a name which is above EVERY name.

Do you believe that the name of Jesus is above EVERY name? Do you believe His name is above heart disease, cancer, kidney failure or any other disease? Do you believe His name is above offenses, unforgiveness, poverty, lack, anger, fear of the future, addictions, sadness, sorrow, hopelessness, discontentment, or loneliness? Whatever name it might be, this says the name of Jesus is above it.

An exchange was made when Jesus was on the

Cross and took whatever name it is we are up against so we could have victory over it. Resist the enemy from allowing him to have his way, his plan, fulfilled in your life (James 4:7). Find scripture and speak it out over your situation and do it in faith. Declare God's truth over the lies of the enemy. Keep on doing it until what you believe manifests in the natural. That is believing God.

Romans 10:13 says that whosoever shall call upon *His name* shall be saved. The word saved is sozo, and it means delivered, protected, healed, preserved, made whole. There is power in the name of Jesus.

We, as believers, have been given authority over all the power of the enemy through *the name of Jesus*. Put your faith into action by using the name of Jesus which is above the name of your problem. As you do this, the enemy will have to bow and flee!

WALKING IN OBEDIENCE PRODUCES BLESSINGS

───────── ♡ ─────────

You shall walk in all the ways which the Lord your God has commanded you, that you may live and that it may be well with you, and that you may prolong your days in the land which you shall possess.

Deuteronomy 5:33 NKJV

There are so many things in this one verse that should encourage us. Walking in obedience to what the Lord commands us (charges or appoints us) comes with three promises, which we will inherit in the land we possess:

1. We may live (have life to the full)
2. It may be well with us (we will prosper)
3. Our days will be prolonged (live a long full life)

The only way to live as a believer is to live unto the Lord. Our lives are not our own, but they belong to the Lord. We have been bought with a price, and that price was paid with the blood of Jesus. When we live unto the Lord, we will be living *on purpose* and *with purpose*. We will not be living unto ourselves but unto Him who died, was buried, and rose again for us. We will be walking and living in the plan that God has for us, which is only good – Jeremiah 29:11.

3 John 2 says in the KJV, "Beloved, I wish (pray) above all things that thou mayest prosper (succeed) and be in health (whole; have sound health; be well in body), even as thy soul prospereth." To prosper is not just financially, but in every area of our lives. God wants us to prosper in our spirit, soul, and body.

God has nothing but good for us if we choose to obey and hearken unto His voice. It says in Proverbs 10:22 that the blessing (prosperity) of the Lord makes rich (to accumulate, make rich) and adds no sorrow (painful toil or labor) with it.

We will live out all the days of our life. There will be no early or untimely deaths. We will fulfill all the days of our life on this earth, and they will be like heaven on earth (Deuteronomy 11:21). I love that! This is God's will for our lives.

What an awesome and loving Father we serve who wants to lavishly bless His children with an abundance of *all* good things!

WHAT ARE YOU THINKING ON?

———————— ♡ ————————

"You Have a Choice"

*Finally, brethren, whatever things are true,
whatever things are noble, whatever things are
just, whatever things are pure, whatever things
are lovely, whatever things are of good report,
if there is any virtue and if there is anything
praiseworthy - meditate on these things.*

Philippians 4:8 NJKV

What do you meditate on each day? What do you
think about before you go to bed at night or wake up
thinking about in the morning? We have a choice what
we let dominate our thoughts. We have a choice on the
kind of attitude we are going to exemplify throughout
the day. The thoughts of our heart, whether good or
bad, will come out in actions and words because the
Bible tells us that out of the abundance of the heart,
the mouth speaks.

If you are in fear, discouragement, hopelessness,
frustration, or anything else that is not faith, then
you are letting those thoughts and emotions set the

atmosphere for the day set before you. You can choose to say no to negative thoughts. You can choose to let the peace of God rule in your heart and mind and think on things that are pure, lovely, and of a good report, as it tells us in our key verse.

You can choose to be joyful and give thanks for each day the Lord has made and rejoice in it. You can choose to be thankful that God has given you breath and life, and use it for His glory. When you do this, you are setting yourself up for victory and blessings to come your way, as well as being a blessing to others.

Make a choice this day to think about things above and not the things of this earth which are temporal and will pass away. Choose to serve the living God and think His thoughts, which are written in His Word and are higher than your own thoughts (Isaiah 55).

Make a choice today to yield yourself to the God of the Universe who created you for His purpose to display His power through you wherever you are. And remember, one positive thought first thing in the morning aligned with the Word of God can change your direction for the entire day!

WHAT GOD SAYS ABOUT YOU

———————— ♡ ————————

"Your True Identity"

Therefore, if anyone is in Christ, he is a new creation: old things are passed away; behold, all things are become new.

2 Corinthians 5:17 NKJV

When you become born again, your spirit man is now brand new and alive unto God. It is perfect and complete just like Jesus, and nothing can penetrate it. You still have a soul, though, that needs to be purified (1 Peter 1:22 KJV), which will be a process. It comes forth by obeying the truth of God's Word. But the *real you* is now who you are in your born again spirit man.

Knowing who you are and whose you are, as believers in Christ, will make all the difference in your life. When you get a revelation of the love of God and what He says about you and what Jesus did for you on the cross, it should not matter what anyone says or does to you. Why? Because you will be confident of who you are IN HIM.

Sometimes your past experiences and what the world has said about you have shaped what you believe about your identity. When you become born again, your identity changes into what God says about you and how He sees you – your new spirit man.

We have all gone through things in life and have had labels put on us by others or even we have put labels on ourselves that are contrary to how God sees us and who we really are in Him. How He sees us and what He says about us is our TRUE IDENTITY – it is who we are in our born again spirit man, which is a completely new creation in Christ.

It is imperative to know first and foremost that you are loved by God - His love is unconditional. It is not performance based. It is not based on how good or how bad you've been. It is not based on whether people have accepted or rejected you, or even how they see you. It is based on His unconditional love for you that never changes.

Here are just a few things He says about who we really are:

- We are accepted by Him as His beloved – Romans 15:7, Ephesians 1:6
- We are chosen by God – John 15:16
- We are adopted as sons and daughters by Jesus according to His good pleasure - Ephesians 1:5
- We are more than conquerors through Christ who loved us – Romans 8:37
- We are forgiven - Ephesians 1:7, 1 John 1:9

- We are righteous by faith in His blood - 2 Corinthians 5:21
- We are holy and blameless before Him - Ephesians 1:4, Colossians 1:22
- We are complete in Christ – Colossians 2:10
- We are part of God's family – Ephesians 2:19
- We are heirs of God and joint heirs of Christ – Romans 8:17
- We are precious to God – Isaiah 43:4
- We are His delight - Zephaniah 3:17
- We are filled with the knowledge of His will for our lives - Colossians 1:9
- We have been given every good and perfect gift from above - James 1:17
- We are God's handiwork, masterpiece – Ephesians 2:10
- We are called by God and created for His pleasure and glory - Isaiah 43:7
- We are the healed of the Lord - Isaiah 53:5, 1 Peter 2:24

Choose today to believe what God says about you regardless of how you see yourself, or even how others see you. Your spirit man is now a new person in Christ Jesus created after the image of God. This is your *true* identity!

WHAT KIND OF
MESSENGER ARE YOU?

───────── ♡ ─────────

An unreliable messenger stumbles into
trouble, but a reliable messenger brings healing.

Proverbs 13:17 NLT

What kind of messenger (or ambassador) are you?

As I was reading Proverbs 13, this scripture was highlighted to me. It is a question we need to ask ourselves.

I love that it says if we are a reliable messenger (some translations say a faithful ambassador or trustworthy courier), then we bring healing or health (to those we speak to). The word health or healing means medicine, deliverance, a cure, soundness. In other words, it will bring forth life and health. There is nothing more satisfying than to bring deliverance and health to someone's spirit, soul, and body by the message we speak to them from the truth of God's Word.

Even in every day casual conversations with people that God places across our path, we should be bringing forth words of encouragement, healing, strength, hope, peace, and life. Remember, we are ambassadors for Christ (2 Corinthians 5:20). There is no greater honor than to be a representative and mouthpiece for the Lord.

Ask yourself today, "What message am I bringing to others? What kind of messenger am I? Am I an unreliable messenger or a faithful ambassador?"

The message you carry inside of you will bring forth healing to those you are sent to *if* it's the message of the gospel of truth - the gospel of salvation!

WHERE THE SPIRIT OF THE LORD IS

———————— ♡ ————————

Now the Lord is the Spirit; and where the Spirit of the Lord is, there is liberty.

2 Corinthians 3:17 NKJV

How blessed and thankful we are to live in a country that has the freedoms (liberty) it has, and it's only because of the Spirit of the living God! As time goes on, and things are getting darker in this world, we can be assured that the enemy would like to take our freedoms away. But as believers in Christ, we have been given the authority to stop him and push his agenda back in the mighty name of Jesus because the victory has already been won. That is why we fight from a place of victory instead of fighting to get a victory over his evil.

We must continue to pray and believe God for this nation. This country was founded upon biblical principles because of the Spirit of the living God that was in our Founding Fathers. It is no wonder the enemy works so tirelessly and relentlessly to take it away. But God knows the end from the beginning; and the end is VICTORY!

The enemy is a defeated foe and has no power or

authority over us *unless* we allow him to have it. But the Righteous are not allowing this to happen. We are standing up in faith and taking our rightful place in Christ against this evil. The Righteous will not be moved.

God is on the move in this country and all over the world carrying out His plan and His purpose in the lives of those who are willing to take up their cross and follow Him daily. This means dying to 'self' and living unto God. Whatever God has graced you to do, do it, and do it with a grateful and humble heart. Where His Spirit is, there is freedom *to do* what He has called you to do, there is freedom *to be* what He has called you to be, and there is freedom *to go* where He has called you to go.

Every person has their sphere of influence. There is not one sphere of influence greater than another, because there is not one person greater than another person in the eyes of God. He is no respecter of people. Whoever God sends you to, whether it's to one person or one thousand, you can make an impact in their lives with this gospel. Obedience to His call on your life will produce God's purpose to be carried out where He has placed *you*.

In these last days, as we call upon the Lord, He will answer us and show us great and mighty things that we do not know. Don't ever underestimate the power of prayer and agreement – Matthew 18:19.

There are three scriptures that I am always reminded of, and they are:

1. The effectual, fervent prayer of a righteous man avails much - James 5:16
2. The prayer of the upright is His delight - Proverbs 15:8
3. The desire of the righteous shall be granted - Proverbs 10:24

1 John 5:14-15 tells us, "Now this is the confidence that we have in Him, that if we ask anything according to His will, He hears us. And if we know that He hears us, whatever we ask, we know that we have the petitions that we have asked of Him." (NKJV)

Know that the Spirit of the Lord in you will bring freedom to not only you, but to those He brings you to minister to and pray for. Satan wants to put people in bondage and keep them there; but the Spirit of the Lord always wants to bring peace and freedom!

YOU ARE NOT FORGOTTEN BY GOD

—————————— ♡ ——————————

Can a woman forget her nursing child, and not have compassion on the son of her womb? Surely they may forget, yet I will not forget you. See, I have inscribed you on the palms of My hands; Your walls are continually before Me.

Isaiah 49:15-16 NKJV

Are there times when you think God has forgotten you? Are there times when you feel isolated and alone? Isolation and loneliness are spirits that want to keep a person bound. God wants to see people set free.

When you experience these times, that's when you need to get into the Word and see what God says and believe His truth over the enemy's lies. In this scripture, it says He will not forget you. Hebrews 13:5 goes right along with this, "He will *never* leave you nor forsake you." God is always right there with you.

Maybe you had a parent or a spouse that forsook you and that's your concept of God. But Psalm 27:10 tells us that though your father and mother forsake you, the Lord will take you up; He will take care of you. He has inscribed you on the palms of His hands. You are a constant reminder to Him of who He has created - a person who is fearfully and wonderfully made after His image (Psalm 139:14).

You and I may go through things in life that trigger things on the inside of us because of past experiences. But that is when we have a choice to believe what God says over our feelings or even what the enemy is telling us.

There are times right before a breakthrough that the enemy will make you feel the opposite of what is getting ready to happen. The enemy is wanting you to get your focus off the truth and get it on his lies. If he can get you to believe his lies (through your thoughts and feelings) over the truth of the Word of God, it will hinder the victory you're after.

Also, right before a breakthrough, it may seem the darkest and most isolated time. But faith overcomes in dark times. Faith relies on the light of the glorious gospel which is on the inside of you. It overtakes the darkness, despair, and hopelessness and casts it out.

Know that God has not forgotten you. Even in times when your faith is being tested and tried (1 Peter 1:7), be assured you are coming out on the other side - purified like gold. Your faith will then come out praising and giving glory and honor at the revelation of Jesus Christ!

YOU SHALL NOT BE MOVED

───────────── ♡ ─────────────

*I have set the Lord always before me; because
He is at my right hand I shall not be moved.*

Psalm 16:8 NKJV

There are times in life that things come our way to
try and move us - to shake our faith. But when we set
(or agree with) the Lord who is always before us, this
says we shall not be moved.

The enemy is always trying to get us off course
from believing God. He will attack with sickness, lack,
anger, hopelessness, or any other number of things to
try and shake our faith and our trust in the Lord. The
bottom line is that the enemy wants to get our focus
off the Lord and on the problems which we are facing.
This is when he will create situations to do this very
thing if we allow him to. If you know you are righteous
in Him, Proverbs 10:30 says that the righteous shall
not be shaken cr moved.

Whatever battles you are facing today, know this
- if you agree with the Lord on what His Word says
over what you are facing, you will not be moved. The
enemy will have no room to get you off course, and

he will have no room to get you off trusting the victory Jesus has already provided for you. When you stand firm knowing you are righteous by faith, you will be as bold as a lion and you will speak to whatever mountain (problem) is in the way and command it to be removed and cast into the sea, and *it shall obey you.*

When the enemy knows he can't move or shake you, he will bow and tremble at the presence and peace of God inside of you.

Set the Lord before you, because we have a Kingdom on the inside of us that cannot be shaken (Hebrews 12:28)!

YOUR FAITH HAS MADE YOU WELL

———————— ♡ ————————

And suddenly, a woman who had a flow of blood for twelve years came from behind and touched the hem of His garment. For she said to herself, "If only I may touch His garment, I shall be made well." But Jesus turned around, and when He saw her He said, "Be of good cheer, daughter; your faith has made you well." And the woman was made well from that hour.

Matthew 9:20-22 NKJV

This was Jesus speaking to the woman who was diseased with an issue, or flow, of blood for twelve years. When she *heard* of Jesus, *she knew* in her heart that if she could just touch the hem of His garment, she would be made whole. She saw it *before* it even happened.

Faith always knows - it is confident and fully persuaded. She *knew* she would be healed.

Faith always has a corresponding action. She did something; she reached out and touched the hem of His garment.

When this woman reached out and touched Jesus' garment (not touching Him, just His garment), the blood instantly stopped, and she felt in her body she was healed (Mark 5:28-29). It says that Jesus knew immediately that virtue (power) had gone out of Him. He then told her to be of good comfort and go in peace because *her faith* had made her whole. You can also read this account in Luke 8.

What are you needing healing for today? Is it in your body, your finances (yes, your finances may need healed!), a relationship restored, your mind made sound? If you will be fully persuaded or convinced that Jesus paid the price for it 2000 years ago on the cross and then exercise your faith by taking a step of faith like this woman did, you will see the salvation of God come through for you.

Jesus is no respecter of persons (Acts 10:34, Romans 2:11, James 2:8-9); He has no favorites (Galatians 2:6, Ephesians 6:9, Colossians 3:25, 1 Peter 1:17 – NLT). Faith is what pleases Him (Hebrews 11:6).

Faith never goes by what it sees or feels. It's an inward knowing, or confidence, that it is already done. *Your faith* can bring forth whatever you need today!

HOW TO RECEIVE JESUS

———————— ♡ ————————

The most important decision you will ever make in your life is asking Jesus to come live on the inside of you and making Him your Lord and Savior.

John 3:6-7 tells us that we must be born again. It tells us how in Romans 10:8-11:

"But what does it [the righteousness of faith] say? The word is near you, in your mouth and in your heart" (that is, the word of faith which we preach): that if you confess with your mouth the Lord Jesus and believe in your heart that God has raised Him from the dead, you will be saved. For with the heart one believes unto righteousness, and with the mouth confession is made unto salvation. For the Scripture says, Whoever believes on Him will not be put to shame." NKJV

If you have not made this decision, I would encourage you to pray this prayer below:

"Father, in the name of Jesus, I confess Jesus is Lord, and I believe in my heart that you raised Him from the dead. I thank you for forgiving me for all my sins through the blood you shed on the Cross. I ask you to come in my life, and I make you my Lord and Savior this day. Thank you for saving me. In Jesus' name I pray. Amen"

You are now born again and part of the family of God. Your *spirit man* is now alive and just like Jesus'. It is perfect and without sin.

Ask God to lead you to a church that preaches and believes the fullness of the blessing of the gospel. It is also imperative you surround yourself with like-minded believers. As it says in Hebrews 10:25, we are not to forsake the assembling of ourselves together but to exhort one another so much more as the day of the Lord approaches.

I would love to hear from you if you've made this decision. Email me at: contact@withapurposeministries.com

HOW TO RECEIVE THE HOLY SPIRIT

———————— ♡ ————————

One of the next steps after receiving Jesus into your heart is receiving the Holy Spirit. The Father wants to give you this gift of the supernatural power of God for you to be able to live a powerful and victorious life.

Being born again saves you – the Baptism in the Holy Spirit empowers you. It is the power source for your life – you must receive the source to access the power!

The Holy Spirit is the power source for miracles, signs, and wonders to work in and through your life – Acts 1:4-8.

The Greek word for 'power' is dunamis, which means strength, might, ability (Acts 1:8).

Acts 2:4 – "And they were all filled with the Holy Spirit and began to speak with other tongues, as the Spirit gave them utterance." NKJV

Acts 11:16 – "Then I remembered the word of the Lord, how He said, John indeed baptized with water, but you shall be baptized with the Holy Spirit." NKJV

Mark 16:17-18 – "And these signs will follow those who believe: In My name they will cast out demons;

they will speak with new tongues; they will take up serpents; and if they drink anything deadly, it will by no means hurt them; they will lay hands on the sick, and they will recover." NKJV

Three types of Baptisms:

1. Baptism into the family of God (being born again; receiving Jesus) – John 3:6-7, Acts 2:38, 1 Corinthians 12:13
2. Water baptism into Jesus' death, burial, and resurrection – Matthew 28:19, Romans 6:4
3. Baptism in the Holy Spirit (evidenced with speaking in other tongues) – Matthews 3:11, Acts 1:5, Acts 2:4, Acts 2:38-39

The Baptism in the Holy Spirit does these things:

- Gives us the power to minister and witness to others - Acts 1:8
- Gives us the power we need to live a life of victory over sin, sickness, disease, fear, and anything else contrary to the Word of God – 1 John 4:17
- Gives us boldness in the Spirit - Acts 4:31

Truths about the Baptism in the Holy Spirit:

- It is for today - Hebrews 13:8
- It is for ALL believers, so you must first be born again - Acts 19:2
- You receive your own prayer language; each person's prayer language is unique – Acts 2:6-11

- It is a gift of God to you that you receive by faith - James 1:17, Luke 11:9-13
- You are praying mysteries in the Spirit – 1 Corinthians 14:2
- Jesus did not manifest the power of God until He was baptized in the Holy Spirit - Luke 3:21-23, read Luke 4, Acts 10:38

Benefits of Praying in the Spirit:

- It edifies and builds you up on your most Holy faith - 1 Corinthians 14:4, Jude 20
- You are praying the perfect will of God – Romans 8:26-27
- You are praying hidden mysteries and wisdom of God – 1 Corinthians 14:2

We are **not** to forbid speaking in tongues – 1 Corinthians 14:39

Other scriptures you can look up about the Holy Spirit:

- Acts 2:38
- Acts 8:14-17
- Acts 10:44-46
- Acts 11:15-17
- Acts 19:1-6

I would encourage you to pray this prayer below to receive the Baptism in the Holy Spirit. Your life will never be the same:

"Father, in the name of Jesus, I ask for the gift of

the Holy Spirit. I need the supernatural power of God to carry out everything you have ordained for me. By faith, I receive the Holy Spirit into my life now and thank you for filling and baptizing me with your Holy Spirit. In Jesus' name I pray. Amen"

As you pray out loud, there will be syllables that come up out of your spirit that you will not understand. This is your new prayer language. The more you pray in the Spirit, your prayer language will become more fluent. It is a perfect prayer language between you and the Father.

In 1 Corinthians 14:14 it says that if you pray in an unknown tongue, your spirit is praying, but your understanding is unfruitful. As said above in 1 Corinthians 14:4 and Jude 20, as you pray in the Spirit, you will build (edify) yourself up on your most holy faith.

Start out studying the book of Acts and allow God to minister to your heart concerning this gift. The Holy Spirit will enable you to walk in the same power that Jesus walked in, doing mighty signs, wonders, miracles, and healings.

ABOUT THE AUTHOR

———————— ♡ ————————

Lisa Staton loves the Lord and the truths in the Word of God that have transformed her life to the degree it has. She is passionate about seeing it work in the lives of others as well.

Her life's journeys have taken her through many trials and tests, all of which she has come through in victory because of the revelation of the gospel. That revelation has continued to deepen in her heart throughout the years.

Lisa was born again at the young age of 12, but it was not until her late twenties that she had such a hunger and thirst for the Lord that He started filling her with the truth of the gospel (Matthew 5:6). He started revealing to her everything Jesus provided for her on the Cross. Shortly after that, she received the gift of the Baptism in the Holy Spirit with evidence of speaking in other tongues.

Being born and raised in Dallas, Texas and living around the area until 2015, she had never given any thought about moving to another state — BUT GOD! He had another plan that would change her life to fulfill the purpose and destiny that God had ordained for her from the foundation of the world.

In January 2015, the Lord told Lisa that she and her husband, JR, would be moving. She assumed it would be around the same area in which they were living at that time. Six months later, He spoke to both of them after attending the Summer Family Bible Conference at Charis Bible College in Woodland Park, Colorado. He told them to move to Colorado and attend the Bible college, in which they obeyed that calling.

After graduating from Charis Bible College in 2017, God opened a door for Lisa to do weekly Bible studies and mentoring women in a sober living home that provides restoration to those who were previously incarcerated. In early 2018, to the present time, through the encouragement of a friend, she became a volunteer chaplain. She teaches Bible studies and ministers to the women at the county jail.

Jail ministry is something she could never have seen herself doing years ago. However, it has turned out to be one of the most fulfilling calls in her life. She teaches women in a very simplistic way that enables the hardest of hearts to be able to receive. She has seen hard hearts softened because of God's unfailing love and compassion towards them through the Spirit of God speaking out of her heart and mouth. Lisa believes there is no greater satisfaction than to see the power of God move through His amazing love and grace to transform a heart.

Lisa has been involved in other ministry opportunities as well, including teaching a Life Group to women through her church on Walking in Victory, having a weekly women's prayer group in her home, many opportunities praying for people and seeing results, as well as one-on-one ministry.

Lisa is a minister of the gospel, jail chaplain, author, teacher, exhorter, and mentor. She is a graduate of Charis Bible College in Woodland Park, Colorado. She believes that her ministry and calling is described in Isaiah 61:1-3.

Lisa and her husband, JR, reside in Colorado Springs, Colorado. They are blessed with two children and five grandchildren, all who live in Texas.

WITH A PURPOSE MINISTRIES

―――――― ♡ ――――――

Lisa and JR have a 501(c)(3) ministry called *With a Purpose Ministries*, which God led JR to start in early 2021.

Website: www.withapurposeministries.com

YouTube Channel: https://www.youtube.com/channel/UCyp7alozwH-FlVYuIwIV6vg

You can contact Lisa

Email: ljstaton56@gmail.com

or contact@withapurposeministries.com

With A Purpose Ministries

COMING SOON!

———————— ♡ ————————

Lisa believes the Lord has put in her spirit to write a sequel to this book in which she will share some of her personal testimonies.

Testimonies of Truth will be published late 2025 or early 2026. It will bear witness to the truth of the gospel and how it works when one dares to believe God. Lisa will share how she has applied it to different areas in her life and has seen His unlimited power bring forth victories and blessings.

These testimonies will be an encouragement to those who have a heart to receive.

~ SIGN UP FOR UPDATES ON BOOK ~

Those who would like to sign up to receive updates on Lisa's upcoming book, please email her and she will keep you posted on the progress of this book:

ljstaton56@gmail.com or contact@withapurpo-seministries.com